TREES, EARTH'S GUARDIANS

TREES,
EARTH'S GUARDIANS

HOW TREES CAN HELP SAVE THE PLANET

VIEWS FROM SCIENCE
AND THE SUBTLE REALMS

DONALD J. NICHOL

Lorian Press LLC

Trees, Earth's Guardians

How Trees Can Help Save the Planet
Views from Science and the Subtle Realms

Donald J. Nichol

PHOTO & ART CREDITS

P 6 Alan Crosthwaite/Dreamstime.com

P 8-9 Honster/Dreamstime.com

P 11 www.rebeccdesignworks.com

P 12 Oleksandr Matsibura/ Dreamstime.com

P 17 Kikkerdirk/Dreamstime.com

P 18 Donald Nichol

P 22 Anna Om/Shutterstock.com

P 24 Mirjohnny68/Dreamstime.com

P 26 Richard St. Barbe Baker Foundation

P 34 Richard St. Barbe Baker Foundation

P 38 Howard Sandler/Dreamstime.com

P 42 Photolinc/Shutterstock.com

P 47 Edward S. Curtis, 1908

P 48 Grigory Bykovskiy/Shutterstock.com

P 49 www.rebeccdesignworks.com

P 50 Wassiliy-architect/Shutterstock.com

P 57 Rondiel commons/wikimedia,org

P 63-4 Flying2Iowak/Dreamstime.com

P 70-1 Bjmcse/Dreamstime.com

P 72 Mike McEvoy

P 76 Donald Nichol

P 83 Noreen Berthiaume/Dreamstime.com

P 86 Nelosa/Dreamstime.com

P 96 Geoff Dalglish

P 97 www.rebeccdesignworks.com

P 98 Brett Critchley/Dreamstime.com

P 100 Andrew Mayovskyy/Dreamstime.com

P 102-3 Honourableandbold/ Dreamstime.com

P 108 Creative Travel Projects/ Shutterstock.com

P 110 Alexander Schitschka/Shutterstock.com

P 112 Sura Nualpradid/Shutterstck.com

P 114 Think4photop/Shutterstck.com

P 119 ChameleonsEye/Shutterstock.com

P 128 Donald Nichol

P 130 Donald Nichol

P 134-5 Peter Bocklandt?Shutterstock

P 138 Richard Kreiger, Gaia Fine Art Photography

P 142 Lade/Dreamstime.com

P 146 Kuttelvaserova Stuchelova/Shutterstock. com

P 153 kdshutterman/Shutterstock.com

P 158 Kuttelvaserova Stuchelova/Shutterstock. com

P 163 Dorothy Maclean

P 169 www.rebeccdesignworks.com

P 170 Backyardphotography707/ Dreamstime.com

P 172 Gavril Margittai/Dreamstime.com

P 175 Jimmy Shroff/Dreamstime.com

P 178 Gert Olsson/Shutterstock.com

P 184 Robert Crum/Dreamstime.com

Archival material made available by: Richard St. Barbe Baker Foundation, 417 Cumberland Ave. South, Saskatoon, Saskatchewan, S7H 2L3, Canada

CONTENTS

FOREWORD

I have always loved nature, especially the wild forested areas, and it is painful to see the ongoing thoughtless and destructive ways we are treating our trees and forests. I was a great admirer of the work of Richard St. Barbe Baker, the "man of the trees," and was looking forward to meeting him for the first time in 1958, the year he died. It was news of his death that moved me to add my voice to his cause and write my first book about trees.

Also, as Dorothy Maclean was a good friend of my wife, Liz, and me, I was aware of some of the messages she had received from the tree devas. But when I began reading more of her tree messages in recent years, I realized that the information they convey about the Earth's older and bigger trees is unique and very important, and needs to reach a wider audience. This was the other major factor that helped me decide to write about trees.

This book contains accounts of many outstanding people who have dedicated their lives to preserving and promoting trees. It also examines recent scientific studies about nature that show remarkable similarities to both traditional aboriginal knowledge and the findings of such mystics as Rudolph Steiner and Dorothy Maclean. Views from the non-visible world of nature are rarely mentioned in any literature. This lack of awareness creates a gap in our understanding, for although the subtle realms are not well known or understood, their activities provide the vital inner support systems that help maintain the natural world we live in.

It is my hope that this book will help provide a broader understanding of the vital role of trees and forests, and of the many ways in which they are indispensable to the life of our planet.

Donald J. Nichol - Toronto - March 27, 2019

THIS BOOK
IS DEDICATED TO
DOROTHY MACLEAN

WHO HAS

GIVEN THE WORLD
A UNIQUE
AND IMPORTANT GIFT

INTRODUCTION

This book is about the vital importance of trees, but takes us well beyond the traditional viewpoints usually offered on the topic. Here, Don Nichol marshals both modern research and ancient insights to show the physical as well as the spiritual contributions of trees—how they benefit in so many ways both the material ecology in which they are rooted and the "subtle," energy ecology that surrounds them and connects everything on planet Earth.

In the midst of our modern technology, we have lost an awareness of the larger dimensions of life that surround us. The non-physical environment is a very real domain of life. It is an ecology of subtle connections that act like the bloodstream of the planet, circulating vital energies that contribute to the health and well-being of nature in its entirety. Trees are essential to its well-being and proper functioning, and when they are removed, these subtle connections and currents are interrupted and problems arise, the same as when the flow of blood is interrupted in our bodies. But the problems are not only energetic, for they can manifest in physical and psychological ways that affect us all.

When people pay attention, they can feel the subtle effects of trees and their energies. They can feel calmer, steadier, more joyful, more vital. Remove the trees, and there is an emptiness, not only physically but energetically as well. Sources of inner support have vanished, and people's lives are diminished in the process. And not only people's lives. The loss of trees adversely affects the integrity and energetic coherency of nature as a whole. In short, the planet suffers.

Using examples from scientific research, traditional and ancient wisdom, and the lives and experiences of some remarkable people, Don draws attention to the interconnectedness of life and the important role trees play in preserving and nourishing this interconnectedness.

When we begin to recognize this, we can find our world expanding when we see the two ecologies—physical and subtle—acting as one. Then we can truly see trees for the majestic gift to life that they are. But this is not necessary in order to appreciate this eloquent book and take its message to our heart: trees are important to the Earth's well-being and even to our survival. In an age of climate change and other environmental challenges, this is a message we need to hear and to heed. Save trees, and we save our world.

David Spangler, Author of ...
Subtle Worlds: An Explorer's Field Notes,
Partnering With Earth, The Call,
Facing the Future, and many others.

ALCHEMISTS OF NATURE

IT is difficult to imagine a world without trees. Since the dawn of time trees have nurtured humanity and almost all the creatures of the Earth. They have provided us with food, shelter, beauty, raw materials for almost every conceivable commodity, and a healing presence. But more important than all of these and far less known, trees are essential, functioning organs within the planetary body—vital to the Earth's life support systems. Without the presence of trees and other forms of vegetation for over a thousand million years, our world could not have developed the complex biosphere that we, one of its most recent inhabitants, now enjoy.

Long before the first amphibious creatures crawled out of the seas, primitive plant forms had been harnessing the power of sunlight, absorbing atmospheric carbon dioxide and releasing oxygen as a by-product of their process of photosynthesis. Long before the first warm-blooded animals walked the Earth, great forests were spreading across semi-barren land masses, slowly digesting their rocky surfaces and transforming them into a living mantle of soil. Today trees and forests remain essential to the continuance of life on Earth.

Anyone who has ever walked in a forest has experienced the rejuvenating effects of the pure, rich air alive with the fragrance of growing vegetation. Though few of us ever pause to reflect on it, one reason forest air is so alive is due to the trees, which purify the atmosphere, absorbing carbon dioxide and releasing oxygen in the process of synthesizing their food. They have sometimes been referred to as "the lungs of the Earth." Studies have shown that for every ton of timber created by a tree's growth, one and a half tons of carbon dioxide are absorbed and one ton of oxygen is released. (We might appreciate these figures better if we consider the enormous volume of oxygen required to create a ton.) For this reason there has been concern in many quarters that the current wholesale clearance of the world's forests, such as those in the Amazon Basin, could effectively disrupt the planet's oxygen/carbon dioxide ratios. The tropical rain forests are one of the last major land-based sources of oxygen, and yet they are still being destroyed at an alarming rate.

One of the more important roles that trees perform within the biosphere is to help regulate water cycles. When water falls to the surface of the Earth as rain, most of it soaks into the soil, where it slowly works its way into the lakes, rivers and streams as groundwater. Trees, with their large and deeply penetrating root systems, draw upon great quantities of this groundwater from deep below the surface. The water they drink up in this way is then circulated throughout the tree and into its foliage, where it is changed to water vapor and released into the atmosphere through small pores on the underside of the leaves. In this process, called transpiration, the recycled water also becomes purified.

Without the presence of deep-rooted trees, the amount of moisture being returned to the atmosphere would be greatly reduced. It is surprising how much water even a single large tree gives off. A single mature eucalyptus tree, for example, exhales 82 gallons of moisture every twenty-four hours. This gives us some hint as to the enormous volumes of water vapor released daily by a mature forest and why forests have such influence on weather patterns.

Trees are also important agents for building and protecting the planet's topsoils, which are critical to the whole land-based chain of life. The roots of trees perform a number of important functions in this regard: they are constantly breaking down bedrock and helping to create new soil reserves by supplying the topsoil with a continual source of mineral nutrients. They draw upon the deep groundwater, thereby lifting water tables and maintaining moisture within the topsoil around them. This supplies moisture to the microorganisms, fungi and shallow-rooted plants in their vicinity. Their root networks bind the soil and protect it from wind and water erosion, while their foliage creates a protective canopy to shield the soil from sun and heavy rains. And when their leaves fall to the forest floor, they are a major source of organic materials needed to renew the topsoil.

If all these functions that trees perform are not obvious, they quickly become apparent in regions where the tree cover is significantly reduced. Without the presence of trees to lift the water tables, to transpire moisture into the atmosphere and to protect the soil, the land can quickly dry out, as has happened in many areas of the planet.

In places where tree cover is almost entirely removed, the alterations to the climate can be quite radical. It is not surprising that many of the world's deserts were formerly forests or woodlands. Even the Sahara was once a thriving forest with streams, rivers and lakes; but its trees were cleared to make way for vast grain fields, planted by the Romans in the days of their empire, thus creating the conditions for its later desertification.

It is possible even for extremely wet areas to become desert. Harry Knowles, an ecologist with twenty-two years of experience in the Amazon region, has predicted that "if deforestation continues at its present rate, the Brazilians could very well end up creating another Sahara."

Amazon rain forest to Amazon desert?

The Amazon represents a large percentage of the planet's remaining rain forests and comprises the largest and most biodiverse tract of tropical rain forest in the world. How would it be possible for such a wet region to become a desert? The answer lies in the type of ecology that has evolved in this area. The soil of the Amazon basin is very poor due to the heavy rainfall that rapidly washes out most of its plant nutrients. The fertility of a tropical rain forest is not stored in the soil, as it is in other types of forest, but in the vegetation. Nutrients from fallen leaves, dead trees and other organic matter are quickly returned to the growing vegetation via a host of intermediaries such as ants, termites and fungi. When tree cover is removed, the few nutrients remaining in the soil are quickly washed away, the sun scorches the open land and it becomes almost impossible for the forest to reestablish itself.

The dependence of this type of environment on its tree cover has been clearly demonstrated in those areas of the Brazilian rain forest where

European farmers cleared lands just before the turn of the last century. Year after year the fertility of the soil decreased, until these farms stopped being productive. Today the same areas are wastelands of bare rock and washed-out soil. Incredibly, the lesson was not learned. More recently, people attempted to settle lands along the newly built Trans-Amazonian Highway; to their surprise, the crops began failing after only a few years. Now these fields, too, are abandoned, the soil has eroded and desert is spreading out in all directions. But the highway is now there and so are the farmers. To survive, they continue moving on and clearing more tracts of forest in order to access soil that will support their crops.

After construction of the Trans-Amazonian Highway in 1972, Brazilian deforestation accelerated to unprecedented levels as vast swaths were cut by logging operations and cleared for huge cattle ranch operations, as well as for slash and burn subsistence farming. It is a prime example of the environmental havoc that always follows the construction of roads into wilderness areas. "Build it and they shall come."

While trees are essential to tropical rain forest areas, they are even more critical to the upland watershed areas of these same regions. The canopy formed by their layered foliage serves to reduce the impact of the heavy rains, while their root systems bind the soil to the hillsides. Both these functions are crucial for reducing erosion to these sloping surfaces, where it is quite difficult to maintain soil cover.

Two of the world's major watersheds are the Andes Mountain region that drains into the Amazon Basin, and the Himalayas, which drain into the Indian subcontinent. The river valleys adjacent to these two upland catchment areas hold approximately 40 percent of the Earth's human population—a population that supports itself by means of highly intensive irrigation agriculture. Having removed most of the trees in the lowland forests, the relentless logging industry is now at work in the hill forests of these regions. As trees are being stripped off the hillsides, erosion, landslides and floods are devastating farmlands and towns in the valleys of Peru, Bolivia and Colombia, as well as in the Himalayan watershed. In spite of this, the logging continues unabated.

Northern Pakistan is a country whose forest cover today is a mere 4 percent of its total land area—one of the lowest in the world. But even this meager forest cover is under threat, for Pakistan has one of the highest deforestation rates in the world. Torrential rains are increasingly causing rapid erosion and landslides to mountainsides and leaving widespread destruction. Although climate change has been causing more intense rainfall, deforestation is a major cause of the massive damage.

As chairman of the government's recent "Green Growth Initiative," Malik Amin Aslam Khan has initiated a number of government-sponsored activities in efforts to reverse sixty years of deforestation.

"Along with a crackdown on the timber mafias, we have started the large-scale reforestation project called 'The Billion Tree Tsunami' to reverse this trend and save future generations," he told the thirdpole. net. "The government has committed to not only reversing the high rate of deforestation, but also shifting the current philosophy of treating forests as 'revenue' machines towards preserving them as valued 'natural capital.'"

North American Forests

And what about North America—the great frontier land of the New World? This continent still holds an important wilderness reserve for the planet. But until very recently, North Americans in general have shown little active concern for our tree populations other than as an economic resource. Is this not a vast continent of seemingly endless tracts of forests? The very sense of bounty felt by most newcomers to this rich land has caused us to complacently squander its resources. We have allowed the development of shortsighted logging and land-clearing policies under relaxed controls, with almost no planning for the future.

Today there are very few old-growth forests still standing on the North American continent except in boreal areas. Even national parks, for the most part, have been given over to the logging industry for cyclic "tree harvesting." Logging alone is reducing Canada's forests at a rate of 740,000 acres per year, even if allowance is made for current reforestation efforts and the rate of natural regeneration. Canada, the land of endless forests, has fallen victim to its own myth and is facing the end of its once great temperate forests. By 1980, Canada was importing railway ties from Malaysia and telephone poles from Finland, while the huge province of Ontario was purchasing seed cones of black spruce from elsewhere due to a shortage of mature seed trees.

Even if we view our forests as simply an economic resource, their management has been wasteful. There have been far too few government controls to regulate cutting and to ensure adequate forest regeneration, while logging companies, with very few exceptions, show little interest in long-term planning. As far back as 1871 the wastefulness and shortsightedness of the industry was evident, as can be seen in this letter written at that time by Canada's prime minister, Sir John A. Macdonald, to the premier of Ontario:

"The sight of masses of timber passing my window every morning constantly suggests to my mind the absolute necessity there is for looking into the future of this great trade. We are recklessly destroying the timber of Canada, and there is scarcely a possibility of replacing it."

Macdonald further suggested to Ontario's premier that some kind of investigative commission be called. But this suggestion, like most others made by concerned individuals across the continent, was ignored.

One shining exception to this sad complacency was the actions of a young Canadian forester named Des Crossley. After World War II, Crossley began researching reforestation for the Canadian Forestry Service in Alberta.

"After ten years I realized that I was writing reports that nobody seemed to be reading," he recalls. "I was talking to myself, and that got annoying."

In 1955 his frustration led him to quit the forestry service and join a private firm. Due to his convictions and silviculture knowledge, Crossley somehow managed to convince the North Western Pulp and Power Company of Alberta that a program of planned regeneration would pay off in the long run—even though almost everyone was certain it would not be economical. Following Crossley's guidelines, the company committed itself to a woods operation planned eighty years in advance, with 15 percent of the logging costs going directly toward silviculture and forestry management. This eventually resulted in an up to 75 percent increase over the annual allowable cut. After 30 years, the company was experiencing a mere 40 miles average hauling distance from timber to mill compared to the 100 mile average the larger companies in Ontario were hauling.

This achievement of proper management is a prime example of what might have happened to the great forests of this continent had there been more foresters with Des Crossley's conscience. "I blame my own profession," he wrote. "All their jobs are now always in extraction, in figuring out the best and cheapest way to get the timber out. Nobody jumped up and down—afraid for their jobs, maybe."

Another factor adding to the destruction of our forests is the method used by the logging industry to remove the trees. Clear-cutting has become the favored practice among most companies. The results of this form of logging are devastating. When a company has completed its operations in an area there is hardly a single tree left standing, and the soil has become compacted by the weight and vibration of the huge logging machines. The former forest becomes an open wound with its soil left exposed to the ravages of sun, wind, rain and frost.

It is difficult to understand why clear-cutting is still permitted today. Many European countries have long since recognized the evils of this form of logging and have prohibited it in order to conserve their remaining forests. What happened to the method of selective cutting that was once practiced in our country? Our governments have altered such ecologic regulations to allow the forest industry to use highly mechanized logging techniques that are disastrous to the forests.

In 1950, when I was thirteen, our family had to evacuate our home because of the rising waters of the Red River that caused the great Winnipeg flood. I spent most of that summer in Sundre, Alberta, living with my aunt Addie and uncle Walt. This provided me with the opportunity to see the results of selective cutting firsthand. My uncle had a modest logging operation in the foothills of Alberta's Rocky Mountains. During that summer, I observed how he cut only those trees that were marked out for him by government workers. He also used teams of horses to drag the logs out of the forest. When his crews had completed their logging and left an area, the forest was still standing, the woodland creatures still had a place to live and the younger trees had a chance to mature. This was a far superior method than today's heavy-machinery, clear-cutting approach, which strips the entire forest cover from the land and compacts the soil.

Today it is estimated that we have already lost three-quarters of the Earth's forests, and yet there is no sign of logging slowing down. As a direct result of "modern" forestry and farming policies, an estimated 75 billion tons of topsoil have been lost through erosion in the last seventy-five years. And if current trends continue, billions more will be lost in the near future, leading to enormous decreases in the world's food producing areas.

In spite of such recent statistics, most countries show little interest in curbing deforestation and, for the most part, are only giving lip service to any action on "climate change." As for the average citizen, most are unaware of the real issues involved and, having no say in the matter, must leave it in the hands of their governments. So shortsighted economic activities prevail, as governments elected for short terms in office continue to sell off our dwindling mature forests to create short-term revenues and short-term jobs—forests that will take centuries to regrow.

Forests are the most important type of terrestrial ecosystems on the planet and are home to 80 percent of its biodiversity, including plants, animals and microorganisms. To anyone familiar with the issue, it is clear that trees and forests are intimately connected with the maintenance of life on Earth.

What is not entirely clear yet is how much of the world's tree cover can be removed before drastic alterations begin to occur within our biosphere. Many of the individuals and groups who are studying this problem today feel that the planet is already at the edge of its tolerance levels, and are concerned about the time it might take to fully alert the world to the very real dangers facing us.

It might take twenty years to establish the reality
of global warming due to deforestation.
By that time, it could be too late to do anything about it,
and climatic changes could have already occurred,
with significant environmental impacts,
such as alteration of precipitation and evaporation regimes
or melting of Arctic ice. (1982)

Dr. Mostafa Tolba
Executive director of the United Nations Environmental Program

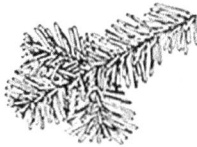

Richard St. Barbe Baker

WORLD FAMOUS 'MAN OF TREES'

OF all the many dedicated individuals working to raise awareness of the importance of protecting our trees and forests, one of the most outstanding was Dr. Richard St. Barbe Baker, known internationally as the "man of the trees." He was a modern pioneer in this work, a man who made the welfare of trees his life's task. He lectured, traveled throughout the world, wrote numerous books, initiated societies and programs, trained foresters and students, helped to generate funds and did almost everything humanly possible to persuade governments and peoples in all lands that trees are essential to the health of our planet. I think it is safe to say that to date, no single individual has done as much for the world's trees as has St. Barbe Baker.

Richard Baker grew up in England within the environment of his father's tree nursery, where he showed an immediate affinity to trees and learned much about them at an early age. When he reached maturity, he felt attracted to the rugged frontier forests of Canada, and in 1910 left home to enroll at the University of Saskatchewan. He spent his first summers working as a lumberjack near Prince Rupert, British Columbia, in order to earn his tuition, room and board. The thoughtless waste of trees that he witnessed in those lumber camps was instrumental in causing him to decide upon a career in forestry work. But World War I intervened. Eventually, after serving with the British Army, he entered Cambridge to obtain a diploma in forestry, specializing in principles of forestry, economic utilization of timber, silviculture and tree genetics.

The Men of the Trees

His first major accomplishment, a tribute to his ingenuity, occurred during his British Colonial Office appointment as assistant conservator of forests to Kenya in 1920. There he was shocked to discover that the Sahara Desert was advancing at an appalling rate, while the forests were being rapidly destroyed to fuel Europe's steam engines, and due to the native Kikuyu's slash and burn agricultural practice. For when the land stopped being productive, the tribespeople would move on and clear more treed areas without replanting those they left. As a consequence, the local tribes were facing starvation.

Realizing that the only solution to the problem lay in planting trees, and having almost no government funding at his disposal to initiate any effective programs, Dr. Baker decided that he must enlist the help of the local chiefs and elders. By his sincerity and personal convictions he was able to convince them of the need to rebuild the forests.

Under his direction a volunteer organization was formed among the native peoples to begin a reforestation program. Members of each tribe pledged to protect the forests and to plant a certain number of trees each year. The program caught on as everyone began to realize its potential, and soon spread to neighboring tribes. Its members became known as "the Men of the Trees," a name derived from the native term for their warrior volunteers, "Watuw Miti." As St. Barbe Baker's work spread to other countries, and grew into an international organization that included many famous and influential people in all lands, the name "the Men of the Trees" remained with it.

Due to the success of his innovative work, Dr. Baker was appointed assistant conservator of forests in Nigeria, where he again began to introduce systems to ensure regeneration of their great mahogany forests. In 1926, he developed a very bad bout of malaria, with a temperature of 105, and doctors ordered him shipped back to England to recover.

During his period of convalescence, he was contacted by Sir John Chancellor, who had recently been appointed governor of Palestine. He wanted Dr. Baker to form a branch of the Men of the Trees there in order to launch a much-needed progressive tree-planting program.

St. Barbe explained that he had no funds, as he was invalided from Africa without a pension. Not to be deterred, Sir John quickly arranged free passage for him on a freighter to Palestine. As he set out to the Holy Land, he was unaware that this venture marked the beginning of a mission that would dominate the rest of his life.

Once there, Dr. Baker obtained the new high commissioner's approval to call together heads of government departments and the various religious leaders in Palestine to enlist their cooperation in founding a Palestinian branch of the Men of the Trees and in setting up forty-nine nurseries to develop stocks for a large tree-planting effort. At the gathering, all his proposals were passed unanimously. Although still quite penniless, St. Barbe then pledged a thousand pounds sterling (a huge sum in those days) to help start the nurseries, while the high commissioner pledged a further thousand. Very soon, the nurseries were being established.

Upon his return to London he immediately made a public appeal through *The Times* newspaper for donations to cover the costs of the new Palestine tree nurseries and roadside planting program. This campaign, along with earnings from his later lecture tour in Canada and the USA, brought in a total of fifteen hundred pounds—funds that were used to plant a new forest between Jerusalem and Jaffa.

In 1930, with a gift from Canadian Pacific of free passage on one of their boats to New York, St. Barbe Baker set out on the first leg of a tour of the world's forests, relying on lectures to fund his travels. He carried with him equipment to film the trees and forests that he was planning to visit.

After one of his lectures in New York, he was approached by Dial Press to write a book about trees for them. He quickly settled the details and agreed to a 75,000 word, illustrated volume. Then, with a cash advance, he immediately started writing. Working long hours in his tiny hotel room, with the help of several hired secretaries typing in shifts, he produced his first book, *Men of the Trees*, in just seventeen days. The publishers arranged for Lowell Thomas, a popular radio broadcaster, to write the foreword. Later, on his *World News* broadcast, Lowell Thomas spoke enthusiastically to his seventy million listeners about the "Man of the Trees" and his work. This caused an immediate spike in sales of the new book.

The California Redwoods

Dr. Baker then traveled on to California to see the redwoods. Members of the Society of American Foresters and the founder of Save the Redwoods League had been urging him to visit California to help prepare a constructive forest policy to preserve these ancient giants, which were being cut down at an alarming rate.

He welcomed this opportunity for it had long been his dream to visit the California redwoods. After spending time among them and studying them, it became clear to St. Barbe that these huge trees could not possibly survive unless preserved together in large tracts. He recognized that redwood forests create and exist within a special type of microclimate that is essential to their well-being. He estimated that it would require approximately 9,000 acres of redwoods to generate such an environment.

Dr. Baker also recognized the importance of the redwood forests for California's coastal climate. "These redwoods play a vital ecological role, filtering out the coastal mists through what is called 'horizontal precipitation.' Since a big redwood will ordinarily transpire about 500 gallons of moisture a day into the air through its leaves, the air in their forests is quite moist. When the sea mists come drifting in over the forests, they hit a wall of transpired moisture and precipitate into rain. If there were no redwoods, the coastal mists would simply continue inland and dry up over the desert."

In a lecture to the Conservation Committee of Garden Clubs of America, Dr. Baker outlined the situation and interested them in preserving a grove of their own. He then set out northward along the coastal Redwood Highway in search of a suitable grove for this purpose. He hoped to obtain an area of at least 12,000 acres. At Mill Creek, in northern California, he finally discovered what he was looking for—a superb grove of virgin redwoods towering over three hundred feet high. In exploring it, he was able to trace life back nine thousand years. Reluctant to leave, he spent that night camping in the hollow of one of the redwoods. From his experience among these ancient giants he decided that it must be known as the Grove of Understanding.

After this, St. Barbe continued with his world tour. On Vancouver Island, British Columbia, he found and photographed what he considered to be the finest specimens of giant Douglas fir trees growing there among great western red cedars near Campbell River, 200- to 300-foot-trees that have since been turned into lumber. He then traveled on to Tahiti, New Zealand and Australia to visit their great forests.

Upon returning to England, he did not report for duty to the Colonial Office. For, as he wrote: "The California Coast redwoods became the most important thing in my life." Instead, he immediately launched a lecture campaign throughout England to raise funds to help save these endangered giants, as well as to help support the work of the Men of the Trees in Palestine.

After completing this lecture series he again sailed to New York. On the evening of his arrival there, he was a radio guest with the popular newscaster Lowell Thomas on *World News*. Dr. Baker explained the plan to save groves of redwoods and related how concerned people in England had given money to help this cause. This nationwide broadcast had quite an impact and was instrumental in generating considerable interest and donations to assist in a campaign to save the redwoods.

He soon discovered that the grove he had chosen for preservation was now earmarked for building concrete forms in the construction of the Golden Gate Bridge. He and those helping him immediately arranged a Sunday public gathering in the Grove of Understanding and informed the press of the event. Reporters and a large number of people from all over the United States attended. At the gathering, St. Barbe Baker spoke passionately of the need to preserve these groves that held the planet's biggest and oldest living trees, and of their great value in the future to people from all over the world who would want to visit them. He appealed to the lumbermen to look elsewhere for timber and to give him time to raise the money needed to buy the trees at their valued price. Three days later, the lumbermen held a meeting and generously agreed to his appeal.

He later wrote: "It took me nine years to create sufficient interest and raise enough funds, but those lumbermen were true to their promise. When it came time to acquire the trees they accepted only a portion of what they were worth."

During the next eight years he visited California every spring, giving lectures and radio interviews to widen public support. But by 1939 the Mill Creek grove was still just a project, since much of the money raised kept going to help save other groves farther south. He decided that he must again mount a nationwide public campaign, enlisting the help of the press. The awareness and financial support generated by this successful campaign resulted in nine thousand acres being handed over to the state of California. Subsequently the Forestry Department was persuaded to contribute a further three thousand acres, and this achieved the goal of a twelve-thousand-acre state park. A subsequent campaign by the Patriotic Women's Club of America saved an adjacent five-thousand-acre grove, bringing the total to seventeen thousand acres.

While in the US, Dr. Baker was invited to collaborate with two hundred foresters from various states to devise a plan for reclaiming the Dust Bowl. European immigrants had removed every tree and shrub and ploughed up all the deep-rooted, drought-resistant prairie grasses on their farms, without planting any trees or hedgerows. When a cyclic dry spell arrived in the "dirty 30s," the topsoil was without protection and was soon blown away.

Once the US foresters had devised a plan, Dr. Baker was chosen to present it to F. D. Roosevelt, who at that time was still governor of New York State. The plan was eventually adopted during the Depression years, when Roosevelt became president of the United States and established the Civil Conservation Corps. This project, which gave employment to six million young men, consisted of planting a shelterbelt system stretching from the Canadian border to Texas. The hundred-mile-wide greenbelt, known as the Great Plains Shelterbelt, was a series of vegetation strips consisting of a backbone of trees, to check wind erosion and preserve moisture, and outside rows of shrubs to act as windbreaks. All plants used were climate appropriate and drought-resisting species.

St. Barbe Baker was not against the utilization of trees for lumber and other forest products. What concerned him was forestry mismanagement—the wholesale clearing of forests, removing all the large, mature trees, planting great acres with a single species, clearing trees from hillsides, and other similar reckless practices that showed a surprising lack of understanding by the forest industry of both silviculture and of the environmental role of trees.

During World War II he was appointed to supervise the gathering of timber in the south of England for the war effort. The demand for wood at that time was very great and Baker spent considerable time and energy in preventing clear felling and in retaining the tree cover on hillsides. He said of these years, "Perhaps my greatest contribution was the saving of English woodlands from complete destruction by Military Forestry Corps from New Zealand, Australia and Canada. I was not successful in Scotland, where the Canadian Forestry Corps had fifty-four camps and cleared whole hillsides, resulting in disastrous erosion and untold damage to the country's economy."

Trees Against the Desert

After the war, St. Barbe Baker, who was an eloquent and popular speaker, continued to grow chapters of his organization in many countries. While touring through Europe he set in motion the idea of an international "Green Front" to promote reforestation, and ambitiously launched a project to reclaim the Sahara Desert.

In the autumn of 1952, with the blessing of the universities of Oxford, Cambridge, Vienna and Sorbonne, Dr. Baker finally mounted an expedition to survey the Sahara Desert—a project he had long felt to be urgent. As usual, there was the necessity to find funding for the effort. Showing typical resourcefulness, he decided to write a book. When completed, *Famous Trees* proved to be an instant success and won him a National Book Society award. The advanced payments he received allowed him to complete his preparations for the expedition.

His party traveled a total of nine thousand miles by car, sleeping under the desert stars, to complete their ecological survey. It was the first survey of its kind and was undertaken to estimate the speed at which the Sahara was advancing on the few remaining food-bearing lands in equatorial Africa. The results were startling. As he commented in a subsequent interview, "The Sahara Desert is spreading along a two-thousand-mile front, in some cases to a depth of thirty miles in a single year. This area is becoming poverty stricken. People who have lived for generations on what the forest yields are now having to cut down the forest to make way for cash crops, forcing them to retreat before the oncoming desert."

But St. Barbe Baker was not content just to make a survey. He felt strongly that something must be done to halt the advance of the desert. After considerable personal research to determine the most viable species and planting methods, he organized and led a second expedition around the Sahara in 1964. His record of this expedition, which he published under the title *Sahara Conquest*, was awarded the Millennium Guild of New York's Freshel Award in 1966 for "Greatest Contribution to Humanitarianism."

Dr. Baker then gathered together the heads of state of twenty-four countries within the Sahara region and presented his findings, in an effort to seek their cooperation for a tree planting program to halt the desert and reclaim it. He also presented experimental results showing that this could be accomplished by intelligent planting of trees. But, due to the political instabilities of the region at that time, such a cooperative effort was not possible and these plans were never realized.

Prime Minister Nehru

Throughout his life, Richard St. Barbe Baker traveled about the world continuously. He moved as easily within circles of royalty and heads of state as among forest workers or aboriginal peoples. Wherever he went he never missed an opportunity to further the cause of trees. On one occasion, while attending a conference in New Delhi, he was unexpectedly invited to meet with Prime Minister Nehru. St. Barbe tells of this meeting in his book *My Life My Trees:*

"Baker, I have read your book *Sahara Challenge* three times," were Nehru's first words. "Now what are we going to do about the Indian deserts?"

"The answer is the same," I said. "Trees against the desert."

"But," he exclaimed, "the desert's only a hundred miles away and whenever the wind is blowing in this direction the visibility becomes poor and the windows have to be closed to keep out the dust."

"The fields must be tree surrounded and reduced in size," I answered. "Trees are needed to fix the soil and lift the spring water table and keep the land cool."

They talked along these lines for some time and then Nehru asked Dr. Baker if he would be prepared to meet the minister of agriculture and the forestry people. He then pressed a button on his desk and the minister of agriculture appeared. "I want you two to get together," said Nehru.

As a result of the advice Baker gave Nehru's minister and staff, food production in those areas increased by 15 percent after five years and by 30 percent after ten years. Eleven years later, when Baker revisited India, he found that similar planting programs of shelterbelts and shade trees had helped to increase food production twofold in those areas.

Biodiversity

As a forester Richard St. Barbe Baker was practical, intuitive, fully versed in the sciences of forestry, and had a wealth of experience and knowledge. He was constantly seeking answers to problems related to trees and forests. While he was on a visit to Scotland, a severe January storm with unrelenting freezing winds that continued for eight hours caused eleven million pine trees on Scottish estates to become uprooted. He spent the next three days traveling to various estates to inspect the fallen trees, seeking a reason for the disaster. He soon discovered that all the uprooted pines were stands planted forty years previously. Strangely, all the trees on the outer perimeter had remained standing, while those on the inside had become uprooted by the storm.

St. Barbe determined that the reason for this unusual disaster was because these plantations were monocultures of pine trees. As he explained:

"The tiny hair roots of pines are charged with an acid sheath to help them dissolve and thereby penetrate into rock. These myriads of small acid-charged roots were competing with each other at the same level for growing space. After forty years, the root competition on these plantations had become severe and had formed an acid pan at the level of greatest root competition. For pines to be healthy, they must grow in a mix with broad-leaved trees so that the leaf-fall can provide food for the roots of the conifers. Nature provides a symbiotic fungus for this purpose, strands of which connect with the tiny feeding roots of the pines, an association known as mycorrhiza. Trees growing on the outer perimeter of these plantations remained standing because they enjoyed nutritional benefits from the broad-leaved plants growing nearby."

Since Baker's time, the understanding of mycorrhizal association has become much further developed and has brought to light some important issues that will be covered in a later chapter. The 1990s research work of the Canadian forest scientist Dr. Suzanne Simard was instrumental in giving the modern scientific community a new and deeper understanding of this vital codependent association.

St. Barbe Baker also pointed out that the needle litter within stands of pure conifers reduces the quality of the soil under them, causing soil microfauna to be poorer and earthworms to be a third the weight of those found in a mixed forest. As he writes: "Pure coniferous forests disturb the balance of nature. Such woods are inhospitable to birds and other wildlife. Birds forsake such areas owing to an absence of food, thus permitting insect pests to establish and thrive. Insectivorous birds are important controllers of damaging forest and farm insects."

My wife and I experienced the reality of this when we wandered into a large stand of purely red pines, planted as a "forest management project" near our cottage in rural Ontario. After entering these woods we soon found ourselves in a place of ghostly silence. There was no sight or sound of any living creature there. Below the trees stretched an endless carpet of brown pine needles, since nothing grew beneath them. It was quite unnatural and we sometimes took friends for walks in these woods so they, too, could experience what we were describing.

Dr. Baker was considered one of the fathers of the organic agriculture movement. As well as championing organic farming approaches, he stressed the important relationship between trees and the soil. He often spoke to farming communities about the value of trees to their farms. As he wrote:

"If farmers wish to increase their yields they should devote 22 percent of their farms to trees—to strategically planted shelterbelts. It was found in Alberta, Canada, that if 22 percent of a quarter section, which is 160 acres, could be devoted to trees, the crop output could be almost doubled. Trees create microclimates, reduce the speed of wind, lift the water table and increase the worm population. If farmers knew how to harness the common earthworm they could double their crops. A worm excretes its own weight in fertile moisture every twenty-four hours. In one year, an acre of land well populated with worms will have 32 tons of excellent composted soil as a result of their activities."

St. Barbe Baker was honored in many countries, as well as his own. In 1977 the Order of the British Empire was bestowed upon him, and two years later H.R.H. the Prince of Wales became a patron of the Men of the Trees.

It would require quite a large book to include all that Richard St. Barbe Baker achieved in his long and productive life. These are but some of the highlights of his work – a work that touched almost every major forest on the planet. More can be read in his biography, *My Life My Trees*, by Findhorn Publications. His life is a testament to the amazing accomplishments that one person can achieve if he gives his full attention and energies to a cause that he loves.

In 1982 the United Nations Association of Australia launched a ten-year reforestation program in that country, an undertaking necessitated by two hundred years of European settlement that had resulted in the removal of approximately 75 percent of its rain forests. In a letter to the people of Australia, Dr. Baker congratulated them for instituting 1982 as the Year of the Tree and for encouraging the government of Australia and other member countries of the United Nations to make 1982 the first year in the Decade of the Trees.

Richard St. Barbe Baker died on June 9, 1982, in Saskatoon, Saskatchewan, Canada. At the time he was on yet another world tour, having refused to let his failing health deter him from continuing to act as a voice for the planet's trees and forests.

* * *

*The fate of an individual
or a nation will always be determined by the
degree of his or its harmony
with the forces and laws of nature and the universe.
The fullness of life depends upon man's harmony
with the totality of the natural cosmic laws.*

Edmond Bordeaux Szekely
A quote favored by St. Barbe Baker

LINKS
WITH
NATURE

How far we have strayed from our roots in Nature—so far that we seem to no longer consider ourselves a part of it; so far that we can happily destroy the very fabric of our own world under the proud banner of "human progress."

These links with our natural roots have been further severed by the way that western scientific thought has evolved. The mechanistic interpretation of reality that science has developed has had a deep effect upon our culture and has changed our entire system of values. Life has become a chance occurrence in an uncaring universe, operating under impersonal, mechanical laws. The individual's place in this new order is rather precarious, for it is a scheme that has no interest in the personal self but only for the "survival of the species." The individual no longer feels nurtured and embraced by either God or Nature.

In this brave new world, this impersonal reality that our modern culture has created, there is a need to rediscover the roots of our identity and to reestablish our personal place within the scheme of Creation. We have lost touch with our spiritual identity, with our connectedness to the Creator and to our own unlimited creative potentials. We have also lost touch with our connections to Nature or to that great matrix of life and energies from which we, and all living things, derive the substance of our earthly forms and experiences. If we do not feel connected to either God or Nature, it is difficult for us to feel deeply a part of our world and to believe that we have any power to influence the direction of our lives. And if we feel somewhat alienated, somewhat helpless and unloved, it is not surprising that we tend to treat our world in such an unloving fashion.

It is important to recognize that Nature is not a strange external force but an intimate part of each of us—as intimate as the air we breathe, the water we drink, and the very substance of our bodies. Nature is a part of our human identity, and to deny it or ignore it is dangerous—both on a personal level and as a society.

In my own experience, I have always found Nature to be an important connecting point. Nature is slow and quiet. Everything is in harmony and simply being itself. There is nothing false or artificial reflecting back at you as there is in man-made environments, nothing pushing you to respond. You are left with yourself. This can be unsettling at first for some people, but once they relax into it, it can be very healing.

Whenever I have gone into wilderness areas I have almost always experienced a deeper connection with myself and with my world. And of all the natural areas I have visited, it is often the forests that have touched me most, particularly those where big trees are still standing.

I can still recall my visits into groves of giant West Coast Douglas fir trees that grew near my childhood home in British Columbia. I remember standing among those huge trees, staring at the beauty of that special place with all the amazement and wonder that are part of our childhood perceptivity. Those immense tree trunks seemed to climb forever upward through shafts of sunlight that broke through the dark green canopy at intervals, to scatter splashes of light on the ferns and mosses of the forest floor. Time seemed to stand still there. All sounds seemed muted and hushed. What had felt important and pressing moments before seemed trivial and melted away in the serene presence of those great trees. It was unlike any other place I had been. Here was a presence that announced itself with a silent power that was both awe-inspiring and comforting at the same time, a presence that communicated images of timelessness and of forces born of some impossible wisdom. No church architecture I have since visited ever spoke to me as did that living cathedral near my childhood home. In that place I felt myself standing in the presence of God.

I feel fortunate to have lived near those great trees in my early years. They remain with me, etched on my memory in such a way that it is impossible for me to think of them other than in a personal way. I enjoyed a relationship with them, an exchange that was nonverbal. To me, those trees did not feel like dumb growing things, for they had a presence that suggested intelligence and dimensions of being that extend well beyond the narrow limits of our commonly held concepts. When I walked among those giant trees I was aware of how their lordly presence filled the entire environment around them. They generated a living atmosphere that was quite distinctive—quite different from a grove of poplars, for instance.

It is curious how our present culture tends to ignore the living qualities that trees bring to our environment, since it is my experience that most people easily sense their qualities once they are made aware of them. A friend once related to me his experience when city workmen removed two mature maples from the boulevard close to the front of his house. Both he and his wife were unhappy about the removal, but since the trees were on city property, they had to accept the situation. Although they soon forgot about the trees, they both began experiencing a difference within their home. One day my friend realized he was feeling a peculiar sense of loss. When he discussed it with his wife, it became clear to them both that they were missing the presence of the old maples.

For anyone who might be skeptical of the important presence that mature trees provide to our environments, there is an easy test that can be performed. Simply compare an area of your city or town where there are no trees or only very young trees, such as in newly built neighborhoods, with areas where there are many older, stately trees. You will quickly discover that localities with new young trees often feel somewhat bleak and raw when compared with established areas with large, older trees. The latter usually present an atmosphere of serenity, solidity and a vital abundance that is augmented by the much greater numbers of birds, squirrels and other creatures there. Real estate values also tend to reflect these differences and are almost always higher in sectors of the city that are populated with large trees.

It would seem that most of us feel drawn to, comforted by and even enriched by the presence of trees. Is this due to their beauty, which is undeniable, or to our traditional associations with trees, or possibly some sort of sentimentality? Or could it be that there is something deeper involved here? Is it not possible that there is another level to our relationship with trees that we do not acknowledge?

Within the teachings of some of the eastern and western spiritual traditions it is held that trees are the most highly evolved form of plant life on our planet. And according to the same sources, it is those species of trees having the greatest size and life spans that exhibit the most highly developed states of vegetal consciousness. The giant California sequoias are one such species—a variety of tree that towers to incredible heights of three hundred feet or more and experiences lives spanning up to four thousand years. Trees such as these and their brothers, the giant California redwoods, represent the ancient ones of wisdom within the plant world, the masters of the vegetable kingdom. It was the giant redwoods that inspired the poet S.A. Coblentz to write:

"I think that could the weary world but know communion with these spirits breathing peace, strangely a veil would lift, a light would glow, and the dark tumult of our lives would cease."

Clearly this man experienced something in his communion with these ancient giants that caused him to recognize he was in the presence of something more than a stand of potential lumber.

Our Kinship
with Plants—a Scientific View

Even respected scientists have been led to conclude, through research, that plants represent a form of intelligent life. In the first two decades of this century, the brilliant scientist Sir Jagadish Chandra Bose developed a series of instruments that could measure the growth and behavior of plants down to the minutest detail. The most refined version of these instruments, which he called a "crescograph," could magnify the most minute pulses of a life process up to a hundred million times. With the aid of his crescograph, Bose was able to show and document how the skins of lizards and frogs behave similarly to skins of grapes, tomatoes and other vegetables. He discovered close parallels between the response to light in plant leaves and in the retinas of animal eyes. He demonstrated that plants become as fatigued by continuous stimulation as do animal muscle.

Bose also found that plants could be chloroformed and anesthetized exactly like animals, and when the anesthetic vapors dissipated, like animals, they would revive. He further tested this finding by using chloroform to tranquilize a huge pine tree, which he was then able to uproot and transplant without the usual fatal shock of such an operation.

Possibly even more interesting, Bose was able to prove that plants contain nervous systems that perform identically to those of animals when subjected to similar conditions. So sensitive were Bose's instruments that when he attached them to a plant such as a fern, one could observe the minutest pulsations and movements of its life and growth. If the tip of the fern was touched by a piece of metal it would immediately halt all movement, only to resume its elegant life dance when the metal was removed. If a sharp instrument was thrust into the fern it would indicate pain by spasmodic flutters. And if the stem was partially severed by a razor, the plant would indicate violent agitations on the graph until it finally stilled in death.

In one of his more remarkable experiments Bose proved that trees possess a circulatory system and that their sap movements correspond to the blood pressure of animal bodies. Peristaltic waves could be recorded issuing from a cylindrical tube that extends down the center of the tree, serving as an actual heart. "The more deeply we perceive," stated Bose, "the more striking becomes the evidence that a uniform plan links every form in manifold nature."

More recently, biologist Cleve Backster's much publicized series of experiments established by scientific method that plants react quite strongly to human thoughts and emotions. His research was conducted by means of a polygraph, or "lie detector," an instrument that can measure the body's electrical potential as it fluctuates under the stimulus of thought and emotion.

Backster stumbled upon these discoveries when, on a whim, he attached a polygraph to the leaves of a nearby dracaena, a tropical houseplant. He then decided to see what effect the burning of one of the dracaena's leaves would have on the graph. To his surprise the polygraph registered an immediate reaction even before he actually burned the leaf. The plant had reacted to his thought of harming it. He further discovered that it would not react to his thoughts of damaging it unless he fully intended to carry out the harmful act. Later, through similar methods, he discovered that plants react to harmful acts performed against any other plants or creatures in their vicinity.

From further experiments, Backster demonstrated that there appears to be a special communion or bond of affinity between a house or garden plant and its keeper. To verify this, he wired a polygraph instrument to plants owned by people who were going away on trips. Through synchronized clocks, the polygraph recorded definite reactions in the plants during the emotional ups and downs of their traveling owners, who kept careful records during their trip. Distance did not appear to affect the results of these experiments, for the plants behaved exactly the same even when their owners were on the other side of the Earth.

From the fascinating work of these two scientists and from the work of many others there has been much evidence that a common bond links the human and plant worlds. Poets, sensitives and those living close to Nature have always known this. It is basic knowledge within the world's ancient wisdom teachings. The aboriginal peoples have always known it and their shamans respected the wisdom of trees and often sought their counsel.

Aboriginal Wisdom

The dilemma of our western society was well expressed in a speech made by Chief Dan George in the 1970s movie *Little Big Man*. In his remarks, the chief was reflecting upon the difference between the way aboriginals and white people viewed the world. This is the essence of his observation: "Our people believe that everything is alive—the trees, water, stones and clouds. The white people believe that everything is dead and so they destroy everything wherever they go."

Although derived from a movie, this perception accurately reflects those of most First Nations peoples, including this Ojibway aboriginal from Ontario, Canada:

"To us people, the woods and the big hills and the northern lights and the sunsets are all alive, and we live with these things and live in the spirit of the woods like no white person can do. For all their modern inventions they can't live the way we do and they suffer if they try because they can't read the sunset or hear the old ones talk in the wind."

And it is evident again in this portion of a letter by Walking Buffalo, an aboriginal from the Alberta Stoney Nakoda nation:

"We were called a lawless people, but we were on pretty good terms with the Great Spirit, creator and ruler of all. You whites assumed we were savages. You didn't understand our prayers. You didn't try to understand. When we sang our praises to the sun or moon or wind, you said we were worshipping idols. Without understanding, you condemned us as lost souls just because our form of worship was different from yours.

"We saw the Great Spirit's work in everything: sun, moon, trees, wind and mountains. Sometimes we approached him through these things. Was that so bad? I think we have a true belief in the supreme being, a stronger faith than that of most whites who have called us pagans . . . living in darkness.

"Did you know that trees talk? Well they do. They talk to each other, and they'll talk to you if you listen. Trouble is, white people don't listen. They never learned to listen to us so I don't suppose they'll listen to other voices in nature. But I have learned a lot from trees: sometimes about the weather, sometimes about animals, sometimes about the Great Spirit."

In the traditional First Nations culture, everything in the natural environment was considered a form of intelligent life, each with a part to play within the whole. Every aspect of nature was to be listened to and understood and to be treated with respect. This was not just a religious belief, but an integral part of their view of reality upon which they patterned their daily lives.

Today much of this earlier Native American culture has been lost and swept away by the total uprooting and westernization of this continent. However, there are those aboriginals who still hold to their traditional knowledge and others who are rediscovering their old ways. They are returning to their roots, to a cultural heritage that one day will offer a much-needed balance to the current North American culture.

The Tenet of "Brother Tree"

The aboriginal respectfulness and sense of kinship with nature is not unique. The once great world religion of Zoroastrianism taught that humanity is connected in every aspect with all the forces of nature and the cosmos. One of its major tenets was that of "Brother Tree." According to this teaching, men and trees are brothers and cannot live and develop fully without each other. It also taught that the tree, being the most perfected form of life in the vegetable kingdom, provides the best possible form of food to nourish mankind, who is the highest evolved life of the animal kingdom. In fact, trees are further evolved in their evolutionary process than mankind is in his. Science confirms that trees have a greater genome than do we and have a more complex biochemistry.

While the nuts of trees are considered to be a good food today, as they certainly are, tree-fruit has come into question. A great many people are currently avoiding fruit because of the commonly held belief that fruit is a "sugar" to be used only in moderation and to be avoided by those with certain health issues. Research had found that such sweeteners as high-sucrose corn syrup (HFCS), processed cane sugar, sucrose and lactose promote cancers, fungi, weight-gain, Candida, diabetes, etc. Since fruit is sweet, it somehow got swept into this unhealthy group. Then, curiously, without any scientific studies at all to confirm it, fruit was declared to be a problematic food by most health professionals from every walk.

There are no scientific findings to show that natural fruit will ever create such problems. Nor will there ever be, since natural fruits contain polyphenols such as quercetin, lignans, resveratrol and other antioxidants that resist disease. (In fact, in lab tests with mice, such natural fruit has proved to be anti-cancerous). Fruits contain high quality liquids and fiber, are very easy to digest and to eliminate and are rich in many health-promoting minerals and nutrients, Furthermore, glucose is the primary fuel used by the brain, muscles and cells of the body, and one of the most perfect forms of glucose available is found in fruit.

This is why almost every human culture throughout the world has always recognized the value of fruit and has always relied on fruit for good health and for survival. This is why the human language is full of terms indicating the importance of fruit—such terms as "fruitfulness," "fruit of the womb" and "fruits of our labors". This is why the Tree of Life, which is often depicted as a fruit tree, is an ancient symbol of fertility, wisdom, interconnectivity and eternal life. Beyond being a source of a perfect food, trees have much to offer mankind and it is in our own best interest to become more aware of the nature of these important gifts.

The great seer Zoroaster understood the vital importance of trees and the value of integrating them into human habitats. He explained that the metabolism of a tree is the world's most perfect natural manifestation of life. Moreover, he held that "a tree is the Law itself," since the life of a tree is in complete harmony with the forces and laws of nature. By their harmonious presence trees maintain the vitality and harmony of a land and its people. Only the close proximity of trees can furnish man with the necessary environment for optimal health and longevity.

Zoroastrianism recognizes that the evolution of man and trees are linked, while their sacred book, the *Avesta*, glorifies the tree as the brother of man and maintains that it is a sin to cut down a tree without planting at least two others to replace it.

***

Did you know that trees talk? Well they do. They talk to each other, and they'll talk to you if you listen. Trouble is, white people don't listen. They never learned to listen to us so I don't suppose they'll listen to other voices in nature. But I have learned a lot from trees: sometimes about the weather, sometimes about animals, sometimes about the Great Spirit.

Walking Buffalo, an Alberta Stoney Nakoda

A DRUID SCIENTIST
SPEAKS FOR THE BOREAL

Diana Beresford-Kroeger is a world-recognized scientist and author. Her keen mind, education, life experiences and sensitivities make her a truly unique individual. In telling her own story, she relates that, as a child living in Ireland, she was orphaned by the accidental deaths of both parents and her brother. Because there was a question as to which of her relatives she should be placed with, the matter was referred to the courts. As a ward of the court, and in accordance with the ancient Brehon law, she was temporarily placed with Irish "speakers," the holders of ages-old Gaelic wisdom.

These elders lived on small farms tucked into the Irish foothills. They were all in their eighties and were the last of their kind. For three years, while the courts vacillated about her future, she lived with them, absorbing their ancestral wisdom and sacred Druidic knowledge, which is closely connected to the natural world. In her words, "They taught me the meaning of life and of love—a love that comes from the heart and encompasses nature with a passion."

Before she left their care and mentorship, they told her she would be the last of their kind—the last of the ancient Gaelic world, as there would be no one to follow her. They bade her to take their knowledge and use it to help a troubled world in the future, for they were aware of a period of global difficulty that lay ahead. They also entrusted her with a sacred duty—to become a voice for nature.

In the end, the courts allowed Diana Beresford to make her own decision as to which of her relatives to live with. She chose to move in with her bachelor uncle, who was a scholar and an accomplished athlete. It proved to be an excellent choice. He had a huge library filled with every kind of book: science, poetry, classic literature, history. She read and discussed it all with her uncle. Having an excellent mind, she absorbed everything and thrived in this environment. The more she learned, the more she wanted to know, and this enabled her to conquer university-level mathematics at the age of thirteen.

Beresford-Kroeger's education in Ireland, the United States and Canada includes degrees in classical botany, medical biochemistry, a master's in plant hormones, medical chemistry, organic chemistry and studies in molecular biology and nuclear chemistry. In Canada she worked as a researcher in flow dynamics of the circulatory system and, as a medical practitioner, she performed open-heart surgery.

With her husband, Christian Kroeger, she now lives on a 160-acre forested property in southeastern Ontario where they have built themselves a house. This rural location is where she researches and works, where she is a hands-on gardener and where she grows endangered native trees and aboriginal healing plants. It is her living laboratory, where she utilizes botany, biochemistry, plus aboriginal, traditional and western medicine, to bring us unique insights.

During her many years in North America, Beresford-Kroeger became fully in tune with the land of this continent and its trees. Her early Druidic background enabled her to gain a deep understanding of the aboriginal ways of life and of their medicines and knowledge of the trees they relied upon for survival. To her dismay she found that many of the more important native trees have almost entirely disappeared due to logging, farming, modern land use and ignorance of their value.

Diana has made a concerted effort to track down and bring to her research garden these special endangered native trees—species that she believes have the qualities to help save us from climate change and global warming. She is focused on identifying and gathering those trees that will be most important for such a future and best able to stand up to the expected harsher environmental conditions to come.

Diana's Books

Diana Beresford-Kroeger is an important voice in our time. She has written a number of unique books about the environment, with a focus on trees. She writes in a down-to-earth style, combining deep insights and scientific research. Most of her work is peer reviewed and published by a university press for all to access.

Her books include descriptions of the numerous important medicinal treasures existing in the trees and plants of the world's forests. Many of those in North America are traditional aboriginal medicines. She is gathering and recording as much of this medical knowledge as she can, for it is evident that many aboriginal cultures are disappearing, and when they do, a treasury of knowledge relating to the plants and trees of these forests will be lost forever.

All Beresford-Kroeger's books contain a wealth of information that will interest the nature lover, environmentalist, ecologist and scientist alike. For example, in North America the American elm has almost entirely succumbed to the Dutch elm disease and is considered to be heading for extinction. She provides us with quite a different picture of this situation. She reports that this has happened before in Asia and Europe where, in both cases, the elms eventually developed resistance.

Now the North American elms are employing the same survival technique of developing underground disease-resistant root suckers that can lie dormant for up to twenty years after the parent tree has died. When they sprout, these suckers can grow quite rapidly, and apparently the majority will show a high degree of resistance to Dutch elm disease. This is important to realize, and we should be seeking out such resistant species and planting them in deciduous forests and on private lots. Although able to grow to over a hundred feet tall, the handsome elm is a very wind-stable tree and is rarely blown over by gales, making it a good climate-change species.

The writings of Diana Beresford-Kroeger are quite unique. Because of her combined degrees in botany, medical biochemistry, organic chemistry and nuclear chemistry, she has a perspective that encompasses many fields. Her ability to synthesize all these sciences, combined with her deep attunement to the natural world, enables her to weave together a great number of threads in the complex web of life, and gives her remarkable insights into the life and gifts of the trees and forests of the global ecosystem. This has gained her wide recognition and she is in high demand all over the world.

Global Forest: 40 Ways Trees Can Save Us, published by Penguin

Books, is a very readable book containing forty short essays, and a good place to start, if you want to sample her insights and wisdom. Her book *Arboretum Borealis: A Lifeline of the Planet*, published by the University of Michigan Press, is most important and very timely. Much of the information found in this chapter is derived from this book.

The Indispensable Boreal

The circumpolar boreal forest is a huge land area that wraps around the entire northern hemisphere like an emerald cloak. It has been referred to as Earth's green halo. The largest portion is found in Russia and Canada, while northern Michigan, Alaska, Japan, China and the Scandinavian countries hold most of the balance.

The boreal zone holds almost a third of the world's forest cover. It has a characteristic component of deciduous trees, but consists predominately of conifers. It is interspersed throughout with vast wetlands—mostly bogs and fens.

The North American boreal forest, which spans the northern part of that continent from Alaska to Newfoundland, is the largest intact forest remaining on Earth. Alaska contains extensive expanses of boreal throughout the interior, while Canada's north holds the majority. The Canadian boreal forest is an area of approximately 670 million acres (270 million hectares) and comprises 55 percent of Canada's total land area. It holds the largest area of wetlands of any ecosystem in the world, containing more lakes and rivers than any similar size landmass.

Much of the boreal is still largely undisturbed by roads and development, but this is rapidly changing. Being so intact, the boreal provides a unique opportunity for large-scale conservation and research. But there are far more important reasons for preserving all remaining circumpolar boreal forests intact, and it is urgent that these reasons become better known worldwide.

"Nothing on earth compares to the boreal in maintaining life on this planet."

After writing this surprising statement in her book *Arboretum Borealis*, Diana Beresford-Kroeger then sets out to explain the many reasons why it is true.

Each spring, runoff from all the planet's boreal forests carries into the seas nutrients that are vital food for the vast swarms of blue-green algae that bloom there seasonally. These microscopic organisms are the foundation food in the oceanic chain of life. They feed the nanoplankton that in turn feed the krill that are the key food for fish and the great whales.

These algae in their vast numbers capture sunlight and, as a by-product of photosynthesis, produce and release into the atmosphere almost half the world's supply of oxygen each day. At the same time, they withdraw significant amounts of atmospheric carbon dioxide. Only the world's trees can match the blue-green algae in the production of such large quantities of oxygen. Without a healthy intact boreal forest, algae will be unable to continue thriving in these waters. The relationship between forests and water ecosystems is a very important issue and one that will be discussed in a later chapter.

If this issue raised by Beresford-Kroeger was not surprising enough, she then states:

"Nothing on earth comes even close to the Boreal's ability to maintain the thermal gradients of the seawater conveyer belts of the great oceans of the world."

The seawater conveyer belts are the oceans' circulation system, which is driven by global differences in seawater density created by surface heat and freshwater fluxes. Their state has a large impact on global weather patterns. These patterns create the seasonal rains that refresh Earth's systems of rivers, streams, lakes and groundwater, which are essential for all life on land.

Another remarkable and unique service performed by the trees of the boreal forests is that of cleansing the planet's atmosphere by filtering out airborne pollution, including radioactive molecules. The needles of evergreens and the trichomal hairs of boreal deciduous trees act as combs to remove particulate pollutants from the breezes and prevailing winds that flow through these vast forests. The pollutants are subsequently washed off by rains and carried to the forest floor, where they are consumed by soil organisms and safely neutralized.

But the global cleansing activities of boreal trees do not stop there. These forests that ring the top of the planet also serve to cleanse and purify the atmosphere for the rest of the world. The trees of these great forests release vast volumes of medicinal gases into the atmosphere. The aerosol-like agents that they emit float out of the forest canopy to be swept away and distributed widely by prevailing winds into global airways. As they travel southward and disperse, these agents provide antibiotic, antifungal, antiviral and aseptic qualities that purify, deodorize and hydrate the air, bringing important health benefits on an immense scale to the plants, animals and human populations of the rest of the world.

Further to purifying the air, the trees of the boreal forests play a similar role in the water systems of the north. In the boreal are many willow species, some trees, others shrub-like. Willows are a species designed to protect any habitat that has water or moist soils. In the boreal forest, they act as guardians of the watersheds, protecting the countless ponds, shallow lakes and complex wetland systems found there. These northern watery systems are a very important component of the boreal, representing a full third of its total area and providing habitat for many creatures, including more than 26 million waterfowl.

All the willow species found there produce salicylate aerosols that act as antibiotic, antifungal and antiseptic air cleansers. As they are highly water-soluble, copious amounts of these scentless cleansers readily dissolve in the surrounding waters. The medicines of this species, which are important for man and wildlife, are vital for the health and well-being of fish and their habitats.

The dogwood shrubs that grow in plentiful numbers in damp and boggy areas near rivers, streams and lakes perform a similar function. They produce highly water-soluble antiseptic compounds for their own protection. But these purifying solutions also flush into the adjacent water systems and help maintain their health.

Many of the freshwater systems of the boreal move very slowly and some are stagnant, making them all vulnerable to fungal diseases. The biochemical disinfectants released from willows, dogwoods and other trees such as alders, purify the boreal waters. These highly cleansed waters eventually work their way into streams and lakes farther south, where they act to protect the native aquatic plants, fish, waterfowl and mammals that are dependent upon clean water. The boreal biological systems effectively filter and purify millions of liters of water each day.

The vegetation species of the boreal region have evolved over millennia and are unique and irreplaceable. To survive in the freezing temperatures there, all the trees and shrubs have evolved an ability to modify the biochemical content of their stems. As Diana explains, certain chemical compounds accumulate in the epidermis for frost protection, and increase as the cold deepens. This enables photosynthesis to occur in the greatly reduced light levels that are part of northern winters.

These unique trees play another important protective role throughout the boreal. The carpets of evergreen forest that cover vast areas of these northern regions act as a passive ground coolant to protect it from the glare of too much reflected sunlight that could, in turn, lead to elevated temperatures and a significant increase in global warming. The boreal forest stands alone in its ability to sequester billions of tons of carbon dioxide and to hold it safely locked in its semi-frozen forest floor. We would not want to imagine what could happen if this was unlocked and released through improper industrial activities. We will return to this important issue in more detail later.

The conifers of these regions are extraordinary oxygenators and are a significant source of the world's oxygen supply. They are special because many are able to grow and perform this oxygenation function in the extreme conditions of marginal northern areas that barely support vegetation. Growth is exceedingly slow in the colder boreal areas and should these uniquely adapted trees be cut down, Beresford-Kroeger assures us that it will take an extremely long period of time for them to regrow, if it is even possible, and they will be lost to the planet for a very long time or forever.

All the world's forests are steadily diminishing. In the last twenty years, 30 percent of the Amazon rain forest has been lost. As a source of oxygen and a buffer to climate change, the boreal forests are becoming ever more important to preserve with each passing year.

Birds, Birds, Birds

It is not an exaggeration to say the boreal region is of vital importance to huge numbers of the planet's avian population. The remarkable biodiversity of these northern wilderness areas provides an annual haven for countless songbirds, ducks, geese, cranes and shorebirds that rely on them for breeding, nesting and feeding.

The North American boreal is a critically important breeding ground for almost half the seven hundred species that call the continent home. During spring migration close to three billion birds travel north to nest there, and in the fall, up to five billion birds return. This region is vital for maintaining an abundant bird life in the United States and Canada, and also of significant importance to the birds of Mexico, Central and South America, and the Caribbean.

For this reason, birders are among those most aware of the importance of preserving the boreal forests intact. Jeff Wells, senior scientist of the International Boreal Conservation Campaign, posted this report in his Huffpost Canada Blogs, 09/20/2016: "A new report released by the Partners In Flight Coalition contains a shocking statistic—there are a billion and a half fewer birds now on the North American continent than there were in 1970. That's a loss like we are used to hearing about from distant history."

Jeff goes on to report that most of the missing 1.5 billion birds nest and breed in Canada's boreal region, and the three species with the biggest losses, of over 85 percent since 1970, are all boreal forest breeders.

The title of Jeff's article is "Many Birds Are on the Decline, But Canada Has a Solution." Now that certainly sounds promising.

And the Good News is?

In 2006, cooperation between First Nations, conservation organizations and involved businesses led to the development of the Canadian Boreal Forest Framework, calling for protecting a minimum of half the boreal forest and applying rigorous sustainability standards on the rest. In 2007 more than fifteen hundred scientists from over fifty countries signed a letter calling for the adoption of this plan and providing scientific reasons for it.

In response, the Canadian government and provincial governments took action in 2007 and withdrew from development a series of huge areas in the Northwest Territories involved in long-standing, contentious negotiation, including the South Nahanni watershed and the east arm of Great Slave Lake. In 2008, both the Ontario and Quebec provinces joined in by committing to conserve almost half their boreal areas— totaling approximately 250 million acres.

Then in May 2010, the world's largest conservation initiative, the Canadian Boreal Forest Agreement, was signed. Involved in the negotiation and implementation of the agreement were Natural Resources Canada, the Forest Products Association of Canada, and nine environmental groups. The act applies to more than 178 million acres of forest licensed to forest industry companies across Canada, which is about 25 percent of Canada's 758 million acres of boreal forest.

As published July 3, 2010, in the Canadian Press: "The Canadian boreal forest is well on its way to becoming the world's most protected forest landscape," said Steve Kallick, a researcher for the Pew Charitable Trust, a U.S. based supporter of global environmental protection. Of Earth's other remaining large forest ecosystems, the Amazon enjoys protection on only half its rain forest—just under 500 million acres—while Russia's taiga region runs a distant third. "And the level of protection being considered in Canada," said Kallick, "would allow no resource exploitation at all on approximately one-half of the land and restricted development on the other half."

With the signing of this agreement, twenty-one companies suspended all new logging on 71 million acres of boreal forest to give the signatories an opportunity to work together on plans for the recovery of caribou in specific areas, and for producing ecosystem-based management guidelines to ensure the future prosperity of the forest industry, and the communities that rely on it. These plans were then recommended to provincial and aboriginal governments to be incorporated into formal forestry management plans.

This agreement is a commendable improvement and sets an important example for other boreal countries. But, according to research by the Pembina Institute for the Canadian Boreal Initiative, approximately 50 percent of Canada's boreal forest had already been allocated to industry and at least three hundred hydro dams and sixty active mines are already in the region. Considering the global importance of the boreal, one would hope attempts would be made to further reduce the area allocated to industry, and increase the preservation of old-growth forests.

The Boreal is an Exceptional Carbon Vault

As already mentioned, carbon storage in the circumpolar boreal forest is perhaps one of its more recognized ecological services. Recent studies have discovered that it is, in fact, the largest terrestrial carbon storehouse in the world. Prior to this, it was believed that boreal forests of the world store almost twice as much carbon per acre as do tropical forests. But these latest studies indicate that the amount is far greater. Although boreal forests store carbon in growing trees, as do tropical forests, they also build up huge below-ground carbon deposits in deep peatlands and permafrost soils. The high carbon density of these regions is a result of the slow accumulation over millennia of carbon that becomes locked up in its frozen terrains. It is estimated that Canada's boreal forest alone stores 71 billion tons of carbon in trees and 137 billion tons in peatlands.

These scientific findings heightened international concerns about the state of the world's boreal forests. On December 14, 2009, (three years after the development of the Canadian Boreal Forest Framework) nineteen prominent international scientists sent a letter to the heads of state of all eight boreal forest nations requesting their leaders to recognize the importance of these forests as carbon storehouses, and urging swift measures for their protection. Here are some key excerpts from that letter:

"As leaders of the eight nations that steward the global boreal forest biome that accounts for more than half of the world's terrestrial carbon reserves and half of the world's remaining intact forests, you have an exceptional responsibility to the citizens of the planet.

"Globally, boreal forests are a key carbon pool that has been largely overlooked in the climate change policy debate to date. In fact, boreal forests hold more carbon per acre than any other land-based ecosystem. The boreal region is also home to some of the world's last intact forests, abundant populations of large mammals and birds, and home to hundreds of indigenous communities. When boreal soils and peatlands are disturbed by development, major carbon reserves are released. These facts make it imperative that the world's policy makers and public now make a concerted effort to ensure that both the boreal forest and its vast stores of carbon remain intact."

Important as it is, we seem to be primarily focused on carbon sequestering, and either ignoring or ignorant of the other equally vital boreal services, including those brought to light by Diana Beresford-Kroeger. Many of these issues are never even mentioned in discussions of the boreal, even though they are essential to a complete understanding of the whole picture.

If we consider the importance of preserving the boreal forests to prevent the release of large stores of carbon that would greatly accelerate global warming, and...

If we consider the importance of an intact and pristine boreal for providing nutrient-rich spring runoff water into northern oceans to feed the vast algae blooms that are foundational food in the oceans' chain of life, and...

If we consider that algae produce and release into the atmosphere almost half the world's supply of oxygen each day, while withdrawing

significant amounts of carbon dioxide, and...

If we consider the importance of maintaining wide areas of mature boreal forests for supplying large amounts of oxygen while withdrawing carbon dioxide, and for preventing the land from heating up, and for their many other global gifts such as purifying air and water, and....

If we consider the boreal's ability to help maintain the thermal gradients of the seawater conveyer belts of the world's oceans that have a significant influence on global weather patterns, and...

If we consider the key role that the forests of the circumpolar boreal region play in maintaining world climate stability and in preventing global warming...

Then, for these reasons, as well as the many others we have been discussing, would it not be wise for the governments of all boreal forest nations to heed this warning from scientists, and not only cease granting resource exploitation licenses, but also seriously consider cancelling a good part of existing licenses?

This is why governments need a deeper understanding of all the environmental issues involved – they are essential for determining effective environmental policies. Perhaps it is time to put long-term

environmental concerns that affect the entire population of the world and all other living things before short-term economic concerns that affect the jobs of relatively few.

* * *

Nothing on earth compares to the Boreal
in maintaining life on this planet.

Diana Beresford-Kroeger

FUTURE HOPE

Because the environment is in such difficulty, it is easy to feel hopeless and helpless about it. But as wiser minds say, it is better to light a candle than to curse the darkness. In fact, the situation is not entirely bad news. There have been some remarkably successful environmental projects in the last forty years and they are well worth looking at. Here are some examples of what we can do to help trees do what they can do best.

Trees Conquer Deserts

Recently, I saw a full-page ad in the morning newspaper for a new documentary movie about climate change entitled *Before the Flood*. The image that filled the page was that of a lush green field on the left half and a scorched and cracked desert-like wasteland on the right. In the middle, standing between these two landscapes, was a single green tree. This is an insightful image the artist has created, since the state of our trees is a primary factor standing between these two conditions.

It is unfortunate that regional political instability prevented the realization of Richard St. Barbe Baker's plans to reclaim the Sahara Desert. He was certain it was possible and had undertaken all the necessary research to determine the best methods. As part of his studies, he had conducted experimental tree planting in Britain's only desert, known as Culbin Sands—a large area of loose dune sand located across the bay from the little Scottish village of Findhorn.

Later, others picked up on Baker's efforts and today the desert is gone. In its place is Culbin Forest, a huge, densely treed ecosystem comprised primarily of native Scots pines. This planted forest was accomplished by a system of laying down cross-hatchings of branches to stabilize the sand and allow newly planted seedlings to get started.

Culbin is not the only location where this has been accomplished. There are many examples of desert conditions being conquered by the planting of trees.

Greening the Sahel Desert

In 2006, the United Nations turned the spotlight on desertification and declared it to be the International Year of Deserts and Desertification. At a UN "Oasis" initiative to reclaim deserts, it was revealed that satellite images of the Sahel region in southern Sahara, taken in 2006 and compared with those taken twenty years before, showed that the planting of trees had caused the desert to retreat.

Severe drought and rapid population growth in the 1970s and '80s had significantly degraded the Sahel's farmland. Poor land management and felling of trees for firewood led to the loss of many indigenous tree species, leaving the soil barren and eroded. With the loss of the trees went the practices, traditions and knowledge that had kept the region fertile for hundreds of years.

In the mid-1980s, farmers in parts of Niger began to realize the importance of their trees and started protecting them instead of chopping them down. Other farmers, on their own initiative, began to slowly reclaim the barren desert and create productive farms by planting more trees. Using a locally developed technique to generate "forests on the farm," they have steadily created millions of hectares of greener and more productive farmland. This form of agricultural forestry in the dry areas of Niger stands out for its remarkable simplicity and impact on farmers' lives.

Each region has its own problems and requires its own solutions. In this case it was the farmers, involved with their land, observant of its ways and aware of traditional methods, who came up with an effective solution—and it was not a high-tech solution.

Due to the chemical composition of the soil in the Sahel region, very hard crusts called "laterite" tend to form on its surface, making it useless for crop production. By experimentation with traditional planting pits, local farmers discovered they could grow trees. This was accomplished by breaking through the rock-hard crusts to dig a pit and then dropping manure and native tree seeds into the holes. These planting pits, called zai, were traditionally used to grow crops. To grow trees, they simply made the holes deeper and wider and arranged them in grids. The trees used were primarily ana trees, *Faidherbia albida*, a fast-growing species of acacia. The organic matter in the pits soon attracted termites, which digested it and created many channels, thereby improving the soil permeability and fertility. The resulting sponge-like material, riddled with termite channels, also retained water for longer periods, helping crops and trees weather the frequent dry spells.

By this very basic but effective natural method, trees became established once more and, before long, began to provide cover for the land. The presence of trees raised groundwater tables, provided shade, enriched the soil with leaf-fall and reduced the harsh winds. In time, the increased moisture of the soil and soil organisms caused a breaking down of its laterite crust and allowed farming to be resumed once more. Other farmers soon noticed the success of this approach, and the use of enlarged planting pits to grow trees quickly spread.

"The results have been staggering," said Chris Reij of the Free University Amsterdam in the Netherlands, who presented the results at the From Desert to Oasis Symposium in Niamey, Niger, in 2006. "Areas that were formerly treeless now have fifty to a hundred trees per hectare."

By 2006 a remarkable three million hectares of land had been reclaimed by this farmer-managed method, providing Niger with 250,000 hectares (618,000 acres) of productive farmland. From 1984 to 2006, production of millet and sorghum soared by between 20 and 85 percent and vegetable production quadrupled.

Before the 1980s, all natural resources in Niger belonged to the state. But after 1985 farmers began considering themselves the owners of their on-farm trees, which induced them to protect and manage them. In regreened areas a sense of property has developed and farmers now protect their trees, and taking wood from a neighbor's land is considered stealing.

But this is not the only method being used by the farmers of this region. In these environmentally degraded areas, the standard reaction of governments and NGOs today is to launch tree-planting campaigns. Yet in dry areas such as the Maradi and Zinder regions of Niger, four out of five trees die soon after planting. Nurturing trees that pop up naturally has proved to be a far more efficient and effective strategy. This natural regeneration comes from what some call "the underground forest"–from established roots and stumps of trees cut in the 1960s and '70s, as well as from dormant seeds lying in the soil or in the manure of livestock. In 2009 it was estimated that this method of farmer-managed natural regeneration in Niger feeds about 2.5 million people.

The speed of the regreening of the Sahel was surprising. According to Chris Reij, Niger grew 200 million trees in just two decades, all due to the activities of their farmers. It was the only African country to actually increase its forest cover during the same period. The ana trees grow very fast, developing a trunk and canopy even in their first year. In two to three years they can reach the height of a man, and after five years reach up to four or five meters (sixteen feet).

To ensure more farmers learn of the benefits of this approach, the organization SahelEco has initiated two projects, Trees Outside the Forest and Regreening the Sahel Initiative, to encourage policy makers, farmers' organizations and governments throughout the region to provide the required support and legislation to put the responsibility of managing trees on agricultural land back into the hands of farmers.

Forests Generate Rain

Another very important result of this "agroforestry" activity is that the regeneration of trees and vegetation was found to create climatic feedback loops that increase the amount of rainfall. Analysis of satellite images and recorded rainfall in the Sahel between 1982 and 1999 showed that 10 to 20 percent more rain falls when land is greened with trees.

It should be noted that the increased precipitation recorded in this study was due to just fifty to one hundred newly planted trees per acre. This provides a hint of the vast amount of rainfall that a densely treed, mature forest can generate. It also gives further proof of the important role that trees play in creating and modifying climate conditions.

Since the middle of the 1990s the average rainfall in the Sahel has increased, but due to "climate change" it has also become more irregular and unpredictable. In dryer years, the farmers came to the important realization that trees are a local "safety net" that can help them survive in times of drought–for when vegetable crops fail, deep-rooted trees are still productive.

The Miracle of Loess Plateau

China, too, has a remarkable project that is worth looking at. Although once a fertile agricultural region, by 1994 the Loess Plateau in north central China was severely degraded due to centuries of deforestation and overgrazing by an increased population of farmers. The inevitable result was desertification, floods, landslides, droughts, famines and local poverty. It had become one of the poorest regions of China.

Due to this misuse of the land, the fine, powdery Loess soil has eroded continuously over its history in ever increasing amounts until the plateau became one of the most eroded places on earth. The Yellow River, which flows through nine Chinese provinces, gets its name from the considerable amount of this yellow silt that it carries. Over time, the constant silting has raised the riverbed and made it easier for the river to flood–which has occurred more than fifteen hundred times in its recorded history.

The regeneration of the degraded Loess Plateau began in 1995, when locals joined forces with Chinese planners and experts from the World Bank to construct a new landscape on a truly vast scale. A major focus of the project was to educate and guide the local people to more sustainable ways of living—a factor considered essential for ensuring the project's success. What persuaded them to join in was the promise that they would have tenure of the land and would directly benefit from their efforts.

First, the impoverished farmers had to cease planting crops in certain areas to allow trees and shrubs to regrow. Hills and gullies became protected ecosystems, and locals were compensated for not farming them, and for keeping livestock penned to prevent them from grazing the hills bare of all vegetation. Terraces were constructed on hillsides to capture water and for growing crops, while small dams were constructed in ravine bottoms to retain runoff rainwater. The farmers provided almost all the labor for the entire project.

This approach resulted in an area of thirty-five thousand square kilometers being restored. It took only ten years for this environmental transformation. And, in that ten years, it transformed the lives of the people by increasing their income threefold, due to high yields of a wide variety of crops.

Soil scientist and ecologist John D. Liu of the Environmental Education Media Project (EEMP) has followed and filmed the Loess Plateau regeneration project for the past fifteen years. His documentary *Hope in a Changing Climate*, which is available for all to see on the internet, has been effective in drawing considerable international attention to this remarkable project. Halfway into the film Liu presents before-and-after scenes that show the stunning transformation of the barren sandy slopes into lush green terraced farmlands. As he explains:

"The high crop yields are the result of the supporting vegetation. When it rains, rather than eroding the sloped fields, the water is trapped by the vegetation in the fields and surrounding areas. The water held in the soil higher up on the mountain continues to feed the terraces below with water."

John D. Liu is the director of EEMP, an organization that films and writes about environmental projects that utilize natural systems. They freely share their information and knowledge with everyone in an effort to educate the world. Their stated goal is "Creating a future without poverty, in a world with intact ecosystems."

In both projects presented here, their success was due to the involvement of local, caring citizens with vested interests.

In the case of the Sahel, the regreening was accomplished entirely by the initiative of local farmers. It was their traditional methods, personal experience and hands-on involvement that led to the working solutions. When other farmers realized the benefits, they too adopted the same method, causing it to spread quickly. It cost the government nothing, since the locals initiated, accomplished and maintained all projects.

Although the Loess Plateau rehabilitation project was government sponsored with funding and technical support, it could not even be started until the local farmers were convinced and agreed to join forces with the effort. Once they understood the vision and the principles involved, it was their labor and continuing care that transformed the barren and impoverished terrain into today's highly productive farming area—a landscape lush with greenery, where people now live in better balance with nature.

Once such living examples are in place to demonstrate what is possible, how they can be accomplished and what the real benefits are, it automatically leads to calls for similar projects. To date, it is estimated that approximately twenty million people throughout China

have benefited from replicating the successful approaches used on the Loess Plateau.

* * *

The results have been staggering, desert areas that were formerly treeless now have fifty to a hundred trees per hectare.

Chris Reij
of the Free University of Amsterdam

SAVING THICKSON'S WOODS

The Loess Plateau project and the Greening of the Sahel are extensive rehabilitation efforts that have had visible impact on the environment of their regions. As important as such large projects are, they are not the whole story. It is a mistake to think that environmental issues are such huge, global problems that only large-scale projects can be of help. We rarely hear of the countless smaller projects occurring in almost every corner of the globe today, whose influence on their local environments have equal importance. In their totality, these numerous environmental projects are probably of far greater importance than we can imagine.

Here is the story of one such smaller and unsung project that I happen to be aware of:

Once upon a time there was a small, beautiful forest of giant old-growth white pines perched serenely on the edge of Lake Ontario, thirty-four miles east of the city of Toronto. It still held in its memory the vast white pine forests it had once been part of, but which had long ago fallen to the axes of European settlers and lumbermen. Although it now stood alone, it was a happy woods for it was much admired by people and even more appreciated by a great many birds. Thickson's Woods provides a striking and unique feature to the shoreline—a towering beacon of green, visible to migrating birds from far out on the lake and promising refuge from their long, tiring flights across Lake Ontario. On some May mornings, birders have found more than twenty different species of warblers resting and feeding among the branches of the trees there.

It's a miracle that an old-growth forest is still standing in this developed urban area. It exists only because this tract of forest had been set aside and reserved by the Royal British Navy in colonial days. In the 1800s, when the Napoleonic wars blocked access to traditional British lumber sources, white pines were in high demand—for these tall, straight trees of eastern Canada were prized by the Royal Navy as masts for their tall sailing ships.

Throughout the 1800s the forest provided a recreation area for church groups who would spend Sunday afternoons there having picnics, playing games and relaxing under the pines on the shores of the lake. In 1919, James Norman Thickson, a local entrepreneur, bought the woods and carved out a row of cottage lots along the edge of the lake. They were initially purchased for summer recreation use but later became permanent homes. Behind this row of cottages stood the remaining fifteen-acre old-growth white pine and hardwood forest of Thickson's Woods.

One day in August of 1983, Margaret and Dennis, dedicated birders who lived in one of the homes in front of Thickson's Woods, were shocked to discover red marks spray-painted on the trunks of the two-hundred-year-old white pines. Dismayed, they at once started trying to determine what might be done to stop the intended "harvesting" of the woods' pines.

Dennis Barry grew up in rural Ontario, where he spent much of his childhood in the forest identifying birds and their songs. This quiet man was a dedicated environmentalist who had already spent ten years fighting to preserve a local wetland. He had been birding in Thickson's Woods for twenty years, and probably knew it as well as anyone.

Margaret Carney, an editor in book publishing, was an emigrant from the flat cornfields of Illinois who had fallen in love with the abundant natural beauty of Canada during a visit and decided to stay. She and Dennis met in 1980 while on a nine-day canoe trip arranged by the Federation of Ontario Naturalists. Margaret became fascinated by his knowledge of birds and kept paddling over to his canoe to ask about different species they were encountering as they followed the river. Eventually he told her about Thickson's Woods, and they arranged to go birding there after the canoe trip. Before long, their compatibility and mutual interests led to their purchasing and moving into one of the cottage-like homes that backed onto the woods.

Attempting to find out more about the spray-painted marks on the trees, Dennis and Margaret contacted a neighbor who knew the owner of the woods, and persuaded her to telephone him. But he was evasive about meeting them, and stopped answering phone calls—including those from the president of the local naturalists club. From inquiries, they learned that he was a developer who was unable to obtain permits to build condos on the site and had decided to sell the logging rights.

One September evening Margaret arrived home to find a huge truck backing down the narrow road at the north edge of the woods to pick up the first three felled pines. The logging had started. Their many phone calls and messages had caused the contractor to fear his plans might become blocked by the growing public concern, so he had quietly moved the logging date forward.

Early the next morning, "gentle" Dennis went over to the developer's house and pounded on the door until he came out onto his balcony in a bathrobe. They shouted back and forth, with Dennis persisting until the man agreed to meet with them. That afternoon the three went for a walk in the woods. All they could achieve was an agreement from him to not cut three large pines growing close to their backyard.

Margaret later wrote: "In the next three days they cut down 66 prime, old-growth pines—they were the worst days of my life. I was working at home, trying to edit a book, and every twenty minutes the house would shake as another huge tree was felled. Dennis and I phoned everyone we could think of, trying to stop the cutting—every media outlet, level of government, conservation authority, naturalist groups big and small. My picture appeared in the *Oshawa Times*, hugging a tree in tears. Dennis rounded up local birders to wander through the woods, one carrying a toddler, hoping the loggers wouldn't be able to keep working with people around.

"We talked several times with the logging operator, a shy guy from up north, who said he didn't like cutting trees in the south because people always showed up and complained. Finally, he agreed to allow us to buy some of the pines. On the morning of the fourth day Dennis and I handed him $1,200 in cash—all the money we had in the bank—and a cheque for $800 postdated for payday. In return he 'gave' us thirteen pines along a ridge behind the lakeshore cottages. Many cottages had several towering pines in the back of their lots and we hoped this row of 'saved trees' standing behind them would create a dense enough grove to help withstand windstorms and not be easily blown over."

After four days of logging, the woods still held about a hundred big pines, including those the loggers didn't want and those Margaret and Dennis had managed to save. The developer then offered to sell them what was left of the woods for $90,000. While negotiations were going on, they drove north into rural areas to gather baby white pines that pop up along roadsides near forests but are soon cleared by road crews. They returned home with the young pines and planted them in the gouged-out ruts made by the big logs when they were skidded out

of the woods.

It was now starkly evident that the only way to protect what remained of Thickson's Woods was to buy it. Still feeling the loss of the big pines, a small group of birders set about to become incorporated, obtain charitable status and then to search for ways to raise what seemed a daunting fee. Three generous birders came forward, Dave Calvert, J. Murray Speirs and Margaret Bain, and together with Margaret and Dennis donated a $30,000 down payment. This left them with a five-year $60,000 mortgage—a large sum in 1983 that seemed well beyond their means. But, as in all such ventures, when you are attempting good works from the heart, good things can happen.

In Margaret's words: "We started doing giant yard sales and pancake breakfasts, and then 'May-rathons' where birders and their friends pledged a number of pennies for each bird species they saw in the woods in May. We sent out brochures and newsletters appealing for help. We had 'open woods' days with VIPs attending, such as the mayor and councillors. We completed the five-year fund-raising effort with a huge art auction of donated paintings. It included an original painting of a red-tailed hawk generously donated by the famous Canadian wildlife artist Robert Bateman. Finally, in 1989 the mortgage was paid off."

And so they all lived happily ever after…

But wait—there was still more to be done.

Thickson's Woods is fortunate to be surrounded by other potential wildlife habitat. To the north of the woods lies an 8½ acre meadow, and north of the meadow is the small, wooded valley reserve of Corbett Creek. Flanking the east side of these three adjoining properties is Corbett Marsh, a significant protected wetland that empties into Lake Ontario.

Across the marsh to the east lay the famous Camp X, a top-secret facility for training spies who were preparing for covert operations in occupied Europe during World War II. It was set up by the Canadian Sir William Stephenson, code-named "Intrepid," who had been appointed by Churchill as head of the British Security Intelligence for the western hemisphere. In the years after the war all traces of the historic facility were deliberately removed from the site to safeguard its military secrets.

Today Whitby's Intrepid Park silently commemorates the events at Camp X during those turbulent times. It is now a natural area that provides many acres of meadows, wetlands and lake views, with stands of native trees and walking trails that connect into an adjoining lakefront park

Everyone was aware that the adjoining properties of Thickson's Woods, the meadow and the valley reserve, when combined with Corbett Marsh and Intrepid Park, could provide a much larger and more diverse wildlife habitat, and that purchasing the meadow was key to assuring this. They could have bought it for $134,000 in 1983, after paying off the woods, but by then everyone felt burned out. For the next ten years they watched as the property's price climbed ever higher. At one point, it was sold to a waste recycling company for $1.5 million—a deal that fortunately fell through.

The arrival of an economic recession in the late 1990s was a great blessing and a great opportunity. By this time, the "Thickson's Woods Land Trust" board was stronger and better organized. It now included a professional accountant, Brian Steele, who worked for a real estate firm and had negotiation skills. He succeeded in purchasing the meadow for $100,000 down, with a 5-year, $500,000 mortgage. Once again, fundraising appeals went out and were answered by thousands of ordinary people wanting to preserve wildlife habitat. Helped by two especially generous donations in the final year, the mortgage was paid off nine months early.

Thickson's Woods became the first nature reserve to be listed in the Ontario Nature Trust Alliance registry. But, once secured, a nature reserve requires time and attention to manage. Projects were organized to plant trees, ferns and wildflowers in the newly obtained meadow to enhance the wildlife component. Every year volunteers spend countless hours helping eradicate invasive foreign plants from the woods. The Land Trust has also been able to expand the woods' reserve by purchasing three backyard lots from cottage owners—lots holding old-growth white pines.

Recently, a passionate supporter of Thickson's Woods, Phill Holder, donated a bat detector and began conducting surveys of many aspects of the woods' biodiversity, from fungi, to mammals, to reptiles and amphibians. He and a few friends also started photographing moths found in the nature reserve, and as Margaret reports: "The Thickson's

Woods biological inventory has so far recorded six of Ontario's eight native bats, two endangered, and 1,035 moth species. Who knew there could be such amazing biodiversity in such a small patch of forest surrounded by industry? We are now working to get the Whitby region and township to join with the neighboring industries to improve the health of Corbett Marsh. That will be our next major thrust."

A pocket of forest in this rapidly developing industrial area is quite a precious thing, but an old-growth forest is a rare treasure. Thickson's Woods was rescued from certain "development" by people who loved nature and understood the need for preserving wildlife habitat. They had no experience or desire to take on such a task, but rose to the challenge and, along with others, found a way to accomplish it. As in almost all such situations, if one or two people are willing to step forward and act, it emboldens others who feel the same way to join in, and then wonderful things begin to happen.

What's special about this story is that what started as an effort to save an old growth woods unexpectedly led to the creation of a block of five adjoining, protected properties that now provide a far larger and more diverse nature reserve for local wildlife. This is truly a happy ending.

May it live happily ever after.

***

Thickson's Woods biological inventory has so far recorded six of Ontario's eight native bats, two endangered, and 1,035 moth species. Who knew there could be such amazing biodiversity in such a small patch of forest surrounded by industry?

Margaret Carney

FORESTS
FEED
FISH

A native mature forest has a significant influence on the region where it is located—on its air quality, its weather patterns and on the vast array of living things that exist within and around it. As is well known, the loss or degradation of a forest leads directly to the loss of countless plants, insects, amphibians, birds and mammals. But what is less apparent is the adverse effect its loss can have on aquatic life—for trees have an intimate relationship with water in many ways.

Forests and Riparian Zones

Riparian zones are the transitional zones between land and water systems that are found along the banks of streams, rivers, lakes and wetlands. In more arid regions, they are often distinctly different from the surrounding landscape due to the unique characteristics of their vegetation, which is strongly influenced by the proximity of water. Although they account for less than two percent of the landscape, they are considered crucial for water quality and biodiversity.

Native riparian areas play an essential role in preventing soil erosion into waterways and providing unique interfacing ecosystems that benefit both the land and the water, and the inhabitants of each. Such areas include the countless riparian wetlands that often form at the junctures of streams, rivers and lakes. The unique plants and organisms that thrive in these wet areas are highly effective cleansers and purifiers of water. Wetlands are some of the most important and bio-diverse types of ecosystems and should be protected by legislation.

Studies show that a high percentage of pathogens and pollution-causing elements present in runoff water can be trapped and removed by the special plants and organisms of healthy riparian 'buffer zones.' In farming areas where fertilizers and herbicides are often used, this has proven to be most important to protect the health of adjacent aquatic ecosystems.

Trees are often key components of riparian areas. One of the more important services they provide to these shoreline ecosystems is that of helping to maintain moderate temperatures near the water. The prevention of radical temperature fluctuations is of great benefit to those native plants, animals and aquatic creatures that rely on such stable conditions. Natural, treed shorelines are also essential for providing the environmental conditions required by spawning fish as well as by hatchlings and smaller fish. The importance of maintaining natural riparian vegetation near the water became quite apparent in those lakes where a large percentage of their shorelines were cleared for recreational use by property owners, and fish populations subsequently declined in significant numbers.

Riparian ecosystems have disappeared throughout the world in great numbers due to human activities of farming, ranching, forestry and land development. Fortunately, in the last few decades there has been an increasing recognition of the necessity of maintaining these special areas for preventing erosion, protecting water quality, providing wildlife habitat and maintaining the health of aquatic organisms. This awakening has led to a recent surge in activities to restore and protect these important ecosystems.

Forests and Rivers

In temperate regions, forest trees are necessary for recharging the aquifers that feed deep, icy-cold spring waters into waterways. These forests also provide the cool, shaded environments that help springs, streams and rivers maintain cooler water temperatures. This is essential for the health of native trout and also for salmon that navigate such rivers and streams during part of their life cycle. Water absorbs more oxygen when colder, and both trout and salmon require oxygen-rich waters to survive.

Atlantic salmon once thrived in Lake Ontario and in the waters and streams feeding into it. By 1900 the salmon were almost extinct due to construction of millponds by pioneers that blocked migration routes. In addition, the wholesale clearance of the surrounding vast forests led to loss of cooling shade, loss of cold spring waters and loss of gravel spawning beds due to silting. Today the millponds are almost entirely gone, but to date, efforts to reestablish this native fish have had little success—a situation that probably will not change until more rivers, streams, springs and other local water sources are once again shaded and protected by riparian forests.

Forests and Lakes

Further evidence that trees can have a significant influence on the health of aquatic life has been provided by the recent research work of Canadian scientist John Gunn, of Laurentian University in northern Ontario. Lakes have always been considered self-sufficient ecosystems, but Gunn suspected that this might not be entirely true. He began studying the relationship between forests and lakes to determine if the two ecosystems were interconnected, and if so, in what way. In particular, he wished to determine whether the presence or lack of tree cover has any effect on the life of a lake. From intensive studies of both systems, he discovered that lakes are, in fact, quite reliant upon forest trees to help feed their aquatic life.

Gunn focused his research efforts on an unusual lake in the Sudbury area of northern Ontario—a long, narrow lake having ample forest cover at one end and a barren, rocky shore with almost no vegetation at the other. This provided him with a perfect location to compare the two contrasting conditions he was researching. Samples of young yellow perch were rounded up from each end of the lake. These tiny fish were chosen because they are too small to move very far and tend to remain in the shallows close to the shoreline where they hatched. For this reason, perch hatchlings provide an excellent reflection of the conditions of their local shoreline.

The samples Gunn obtained showed a remarkable difference between the two populations. Those taken from the forested end were up to four

times larger than those taken from the treeless end. But more surprising were the results from the lab analysis of the perch. It revealed that up to 70 percent of their food came from trees—a far higher percentage than anyone had expected.

The next question that needed to be answered was in what way are trees feeding fish? It quickly became apparent that the answer was to be found in their leaves. Tree leaves that fall or are blown into a lake soon sink into the water, where they quickly become colonized with bacteria. The aquatic bacteria that eat the leaves are then consumed by zooplankton, and they in turn are a key food for smaller fish. While larger lake fish, such as bass and trout, also feed on zooplankton, small fish such as perch are an important menu item for them as well. Therefore, trees play a primary role in feeding the lake's entire fish population.

Forests and Seas

The important relationship between forests and aquatic ecosystems is not limited to those that are fresh water. It is also true for oceans and seas. As previously discussed, runoff waters from the planet's boreal forests carry nutrients into the seas that are essential to the life of these arctic waters. Most importantly, nutrients in the boreal spring runoff are vital for feeding the vast swarms of blue-green algae that bloom there seasonally. These microscopic organisms are the foundation food in the oceanic chain of life.

For anyone requiring hard evidence of the important relationship between forests and marine life, there is a well-documented example contained in a recent film co-written by Diana Beresford-Kroeger entitled *Call of the Forest—The Forgotten Wisdom of Trees* (available online.) A segment of her film describes an event that occurred over a century ago on the Erimo peninsula of the Japanese island of Hokkaido, where the marine ecosystem suddenly collapsed and died along a thousand kilometers of coastline. Although no one could explain why it had happened, many suspected it was due to deforestation.

Prior to the collapse of the fishery, Japanese settlers had cleared the entire peninsula of its native forest trees to create farmland. Without the protection of the trees, the rich forest humus layer dried out and was gradually blown away by the strong prevailing winds that sweep across the peninsula almost daily. Before long, the area became a desert—a barren ecosystem devoid of any growing thing. Unfortunately, the desertification didn't stop at the water's edge, but continued to spread into the ecosystem of the sea.

It is only in recent years that the reason for the collapse of the marine ecosystem has become clear, thanks to the research work of Japanese professor Katsuhiko Matsunaga. The professor had been researching a basic problem related to marine plant growth. Realizing that the iron molecule lies at the heart of the marine food chain and that photosynthetic marine plants are unable to absorb iron in its natural state, Matsunaga was focusing his research on finding the form of iron that marine plants are able to absorb. Eventually he discovered that it can be found in fulvic acid—a compound that is naturally created by decaying plant materials such as dead and fallen trees, branches and leaves. The rich humus of a forest floor is a major source of fulvic acid. This water-soluble substance, containing iron as well as nitrogen, phosphorous, silica, and other nutrients, is required by marine plants to grow and thrive. The fulvic acid holding these nutrients is released from the forest humus by the dissolving action of rain, and then carried into the sea by runoff water, streams and rivers.

Professor Matsunaga's important work has provided scientific evidence of a direct link between forests and marine ecosystems. As knowledge of this vital connection became better known, Japanese fishermen began to demand that forests in coastal areas be replanted and preserved. These riparian forests have become known locally as "fishermen's forests."

The relationship between forests and aquatic ecosystems is yet another example of how interrelated everything is in the natural world. There are countless such interdependent relationships to be found in nature throughout the planet, and scientists today are quite involved in discovering and understanding them.

DOROTHY MACLEAN
VOICES FROM NATURE

Dorothy Maclean was born January 7, 1920, in Guelph, Ontario, where she spent many of her childhood days exploring the woods adjoining her home. By the time she had completed her education and graduated from the University of Western Ontario, World War II had broken out. Through a series of unusual events, Dorothy found her way into the employment of the British Intelligence Services for the western hemisphere, headed by the Canadian William Stephenson, who had been appointed by Winston Churchill and given the code name "Intrepid." Throughout the duration of the war, her work with the SIS took her first to New York, then to South America and finally to London, England.

She left the SIS after the war and decided to remain in England, where she embarked upon a period of inner exploration, seeking answers to the larger questions of life. This eventually brought her into the company of like-minded people with background experiences in various spiritual groups. Two of these, Eileen and Peter Caddy, had the same spiritual mentor as Dorothy—a sensitive named Sheena, whom they all respected and trusted. Over a number of years, Sheena taught them to listen deeply and to trust their intuition and inner guidance.

Like others within this group, Dorothy made a practice of sitting quietly each day, to attune to an inner presence, an inspirational source that she experienced as her inner divinity. During these quiet times, as her meditations deepened, she began receiving inner communications, which she put into her own words and wrote down in shorthand while receiving them. At first she was very distrustful of these communications, but Sheena examined them and assured her that the messages were not imaginary, and encouraged her to continue developing this skill. Sheena also told Dorothy, Eileen and Peter that they had an important spiritual work to do together in the future, one that she would not be a part of.

Eventually, they needed to secure a source of income, and Peter found an employment opportunity in northern Scotland. The three of them then moved there to manage a once-famous summer spa, the Cluny Hill Hotel. They quietly ran it on spiritual principles and this proved to be so effective that they were able to turn it into a successful operation. At the end of the season, the management decided to move them to another of their hotels. But they were not as successful there and were suddenly given four hours' notice to leave by the local general manager, who was quite opposed to their methods of management. Now unemployed and with very little funds, Dorothy, Eileen and Peter, plus the Caddys' three young sons, moved into an old mobile home in a trailer park sited on a patch of sand and gravel on Findhorn Bay in northern Scotland.

Over the long nights and short days of winter, Peter began studying gardening books to try and understand what he must do to create a garden for their needs in the poor local soil. But he could not find any information relating to the bleak conditions facing him. Little did the group know that they were now located in the spot where they would become instrumental in developing the world-famous Findhorn garden.

Attuning to the Forces of Nature

In the spring of 1962 Dorothy received an inner directive during a meditation suggesting that she attune to the "forces of nature." When she discussed this message with the group, they supported the idea, and Peter suggested that attuning to the forces of Nature might help them with the development of the vegetable garden he was planning. But Dorothy still felt unsure about it and hesitant to try. One day, during a meditation when she was feeling quite centered and clear, she decided to attempt the attunement and received the following inner response:

Yes, you can cooperate in the garden. Begin by thinking about the nature spirits, the higher overlighting nature spirits, and tune in to them. That will be so unusual as to draw their interest here. They will be overjoyed to find some members of the human family eager for their help. This is the first step. By the higher nature spirits I mean the spirits of differing physical forms such as clouds, rain and plants. The smaller individual nature spirits are under their jurisdiction.

In the new world to come these realms will be open to humans—or I should say, humans will be open to them. Just be open and seek into the glorious realms of Nature with sympathy and understanding, knowing that these beings are of the Light, willing to help but suspicious of humans and on the lookout for the false. Keep with me and they will not find it, and you will all build toward the new.

In spite of all the encouragement from her inner source and her friends, Dorothy still feared it might be an illusion. She was a down-to-earth person who tended to question everything, and the idea of contacting higher nature spirits seemed a feat much beyond her capabilities, so she kept putting off any attempt. But one morning during her inner attunement she found herself "within a stream of power" that made her feel capable of attempting it.

The problem facing her was where to start and how to proceed. It came to her that if there is a higher intelligence that infuses a particular plant, then the same plant must embody qualities that reflect the essence of that intelligence. In other words, the outer form must give some hint of its inner essence.

To test this approach, Dorothy decided to select a plant she was quite familiar with—her favorite vegetable, the common garden pea. She then began to focus on all its qualities, its shape, color, texture, smell and taste. All this she did while still holding a high state of attunement. To her surprise, she made an immediate link with an intelligent presence that communicated to her with directness and lucidity:

I can speak to you, human. Though I am entirely involved in my work, you have come straight into my awareness. My work is clear before me: to bring the force fields into manifestation in conformance to the patterns regardless of obstacles, of which there are many on this man-infested world. While the vegetable kingdom holds no grudge against those it feeds, man takes what he can as a matter of course, giving no thanks, which to us is a strange response.

What I would tell you is that we are entirely aligned with our work, never deviating from our course for one moment in all our thoughts, feelings and actions. You could forge ahead in the same way. But humans generally don't seem to know where they are going or why. If they did, what powerful beings they would be! If they were on the right course, how we could cooperate with them! I bid you farewell.

Dorothy's friends were delighted with the success of her attunements and, in the following days, Peter began suggesting gardening questions for her to pose. Any suggestions or information received by her was then put directly to the test in their new garden. Whenever gardening questions or difficulties arose, Dorothy would attune to the overlighting intelligence of the relevant vegetable and present the problem. All the suggestions she received from them were always harmonious with the ways of nature, and when Peter applied them in his gardening work, they always proved to be quite effective.

This was not the only way in which these subtle beings were involved. Due to the group's openness to them and appreciation for their work, the devas were able to cooperate more fully by directing forces to the garden plants to enhance their vitality.

Out of this direct cooperation with nature emerged an unusually splendid garden, in spite of its unlikely location—a sand dune on the coast of northern Scotland that supported only gorse and a coarse grass. In time, news of the outstanding vigor and bounty of the garden began to spread and to draw attention. Many curious visitors began to show up to see it for themselves—first, from the British Isles and later, from all over the globe. In time, due to the remarkable success of the garden and the vision and vitality of the group, a community grew up around them and their activities. This community became established as the Findhorn Foundation, which for many years generated a great deal of interest throughout the world.

Intelligences of Nature

After her initial contacts with these nature beings, many questions were raised in Dorothy's mind. Who were they? What were they like? She soon realized that she was not communicating with the spirit of an individual plant but with an intelligence that seemed to infuse every plant of its species. It became clear to her that every type of plant was overlighted by its own "species intelligence" or "group soul"—an intelligence that held within its consciousness the archetypal pattern for the species under its care and wielded universal energies to bring that pattern into physical manifestation. They seemed to function outside of time and space and could be found active at any moment within each individual plant of that species, regardless of its location on the planet. The understanding that Dorothy eventually arrived at is best summed up in her own words:

"A slight acquaintance with theosophical literature, together with my own intuition that was prompted by the tremendous purity, joy and praise that seemed to emanate from these beings, led me to conclude that they were some type of angel. As the word *angel* had a very restricted and stereotyped image in my mind that seemed contrary to the impression of lightness, freedom and formlessness given by these beings, I decided to call them 'devas,' a Sanskrit word meaning 'shining ones.' The word was no doubt used often in India, but it was not hackneyed or conventional in my mind."

In one communication these subtle beings tried to give Dorothy insight into their nature:

We, as overseeing causative forces of manifestation, would share with you a little of our consciousness. Everything manifest is in our care, and we know its state, for under God we make plain His creation. All is in our consciousness. Consciousness is an open book for all to share with us, for we are so much one that what we know is not separate from what our neighbor knows.

How can we wholly express the light and loving intention of all creation, the sparkling dynamic purpose of perfection, which is the motive of all that is, some small part of which goes through our hands?

In all this we are absolutely and utterly free. There is no freedom unless one is completely part of all; until then freedom is limited. For all are one, and if any believe otherwise, they are circumscribing their part in the whole and imprisoning themselves in the part.

You may have a garden in your care, and on looking in on it one day you find that, unknown to you, certain growth has occurred. But we know all at once and nothing is closed to us. Our consciousness is like a dipping into a sea of knowing, for all forces are connected, as if a loving computer links all because all cannot otherwise be. You have to be whole to see the whole; until then, parts have to be seen separately. We see wholly with regard to our work.

In another of Dorothy's attunements she found herself in contact with what she decided was a "landscape deva," an intelligence that presided over and worked with the energies and forces of a particular area of land that included the Findhorn garden. (She later discovered intelligences that presided over larger regions and even entire countries.) This landscape deva explained that it functioned as a director of streams of cosmic energy to the Earth, not just for plant growth but for many purposes, such as relaying energies from the stars while working to balance and refine them. She decided that such intelligences must act as conscious power stations.

Enter the Trees

One morning, during the early days of the Findhorn garden, Dorothy decided to attune to the deva of a tree. The only trees growing near where they were living at that time was a group of native Scots pines that had been planted to form a shelterbelt. In her first contact with a tree deva she immediately felt a presence of a different quality from those of garden plants. There was a strong and solid feeling emanating from this deva that was quite different from all others. Within this first communication from the intelligence of a tree were the threads of a message that would be repeated many times by devas of other trees.

We are guardians of the Earth in many ways, and humans should be a part of what we guard. We are not active young things; we are, in many ways, like a school of benevolent philosophers with unhuman purity and a great wish to serve humanity. Trees are vital to man and to life on this planet, and we are eager to experience this contact with some of you humans before the others of your kind destroy all that trees have built up.

Of the many different types of devas that Dorothy contacted, only tree devas had such an urgent message that they were anxious to convey to mankind. Dorothy evidently offered them a unique opportunity for reaching out to mankind to explain their concerns. Often these communications would emphasize the need for preserving what was left of the older and larger trees, making it clear that old-growth trees were essential for the protection and well-being of the planet.

Here is a portion of a message Dorothy received when she attuned to the deva of a newly planted Monterey Cypress to welcome it into their garden—a message that surprised her by its intensity.

We enter with a lordly sweep, for we are not just the small trees you see in your garden, but denizens of great hills in the sun and wind. We put up with being hedges, but always in our inner being is a longing to be fully ourselves in the open sun-kissed places where we stand in clustered grandeur.

We of the plant world have our pattern and our destiny, and feel it quite wrong that because of human encroachment we, and others like us, are not allowed to be what we truly are. We have our part to fulfill in the scheme of things. We have been nurtured for this very reason, and now, in this age, many of us can only dream of the open spaces where we can fulfill ourselves. The pattern is ever before us, out of reach, a dream we are ever growing toward but seldom obtaining. We are not a mistake on the part of Nature. We have our work to do.

Humanity is becoming controller of the world's forests and is just beginning to realize how much forests are needed. But you cover acres with one quick-growing species, selecting trees for foolish economic reasons with no awareness at all of the planet's real needs. This shows utter ignorance of the purpose of trees and their channeling of diverse universal forces. Perhaps if humans were in tune with the universe, as we are, they would realize that the world needs us on a large scale. But at present the planet is being denied what it now needs more than ever—the forces that come through the mature and stately trees.

It should be understood that although Dorothy faithfully wrote down in shorthand all deva communications as she received them, their messages were "impressions" and their meaning had to be translated into her own words. Even though their thoughts were clothed in her words, there is a difference in the quality, style and tone of them when compared with Dorothy's normal writing.

You can verify this and learn much more about Dorothy Maclean's life and experiences in her very readable and popular biography *To Hear the Angels Sing*, published by Lorian Press LLC. Those who have read Dorothy's personal story as well as those who have attended her talks are often surprised to find that she is, in fact, a very "down to earth" person.

The Message of the Trees

Dorothy's messages from tree devas range over a period of many long years and include communications from a wide variety of species, from mountain ash to California redwoods. In order to reduce repetition and the space required to include each of these messages in their entirety, I have selected excerpts from those that reflect one of their most consistent themes and have organized them into a single group of communications. This is quite appropriate, since devas have a shared consciousness and any one can speak for all others.

The following group of messages, received from various tree devas over the years, relate to their most urgent concern—the plight of the planet's large, mature trees:

Large trees are essential to the well-being of the Earth. No other can do the job they do. They and humanity each represent the apex of a particular form of life and humans could gain much by association with them. It is no accident that the Buddha is said to have found enlightenment under a tree. It would be most beneficial if large woodlands were retained near every city, for trees have a special gift to offer man in this age of speed and change. They embody the qualities of strength, stability and continuity. They bless all who come and rest within their aura.

Large trees are conductors of energy; they stand ever ready, channeling the universal forces that surround and are part of the world. These trees are carriers of especially potent vibrations, sentinels of cosmic energy, transforming this power and conducting it into the Earth.

Humans are despoiling the power of trees on Earth. Nowhere is this more pronounced than in the thoughtless felling of the ancient trees. It cannot be emphasized too much that these tall trees are needed. It is not enough to reforest the land, for young trees are not capable of conducting the higher planetary energies; only mature trees can fulfill this task. You cannot expect a child to perform the tasks of an adult.

Nature is not a blind force; it is conscious and has inner vehicles. There have been mighty changes in the past as this Earth has evolved, but as long as the sun shines and life depends on water, large trees will remain necessary. This is not merely because they control rainfall, but they also draw forth inner radiances which are as necessary to the land as rain. It is important for man to realize that the natural environment is full of forces that correspond to and therefore can bring out, through resonance, some part of his own nature. Man is deeply influenced by his environment in many subtle yet profound ways.

Mature trees are needed within all environments for the balance of peace and stability that they embody. Their serene strength provides an aura of groundedness and upliftment to all life throughout the world. Where there is a dearth of large trees, the peace and stability of mankind is also affected, for all lives are deeply connected. Trees and humans are blood brothers, made from the same substance, each fulfilling his destiny on this planet. They are interdependent, and therefore man must come to understand that he cannot destroy trees without also bringing destruction to himself.

The basic message of these communications echoes the concerns raised by many people today, including those who work with nature in a professional capacity, such as foresters, environmental scientists and ecologists. All these voices speak of the same concern—of the plight of our planet due to its rapidly shrinking forests, and in particular, its old-growth forests. It is an issue that needs to be taken seriously, and one that requires action.

* * *

Great forests must flourish and humanity must see
to this if they wish to continue to live on this planet.
The knowledge of this necessity must become a part of human
consciousness, as evident as the need for water. Trees function
like the skin of the Earth, and a skin not only covers and
protects, but also passes through it the forces of life.
Nothing could be more vital to
the life of the planet than trees.

Leyland Cypress deva, Sept 14, 1969

INNER REALMS
OF NATURE:
NATURE SPIRITS AND DEVAS

In olden times our ancestors on all continents lived close to nature and were more open to its ways and more aware of the non-physical realms or "near worlds." They were aware of and respectful of nature spirits and the great spirits of the trees. They were aware also of places in nature that held special powers and should be respected, and in some cases, left alone. There were some who worshipped in the uplifting atmosphere of sacred groves and a great many who revered nature and saw it as a reflection of the Creator's hand.

As Christianity emerged in the western world, its leaders began to view these earlier nature-oriented religions as a barrier to the spread of its message, and as the church grew in power, it worked with dedication to tear people away from these earlier forms of worship. So instead of becoming integrated into Christianity, a reverence for nature was deemed sinful and became forbidden. And when Europeans conquered and colonized other lands, the same attitude was forced upon local indigenous peoples. In the western world, the church has played a significant role in turning people away from their roots in nature.

Then, in the thirteenth century, a new champion arose. Science stepped forward and declared that if something couldn't be measured with the five human senses, it must be "non-sense," imagination or superstition. This is difficult to counter, since how can anyone verify what we experience with our finer senses?

It is true that the emergence of the scientific age was a breath of fresh air that helped free a world congested with restricting beliefs, and opened up new directions. But, by accepting a scientific view of our world with such devotion, we have succeeded in throwing out the baby with the bathwater. Where religion did a good job in turning us away from nature, science did a fine job of causing us to distrust our gut feelings, our common sense and our intuitions that connect us with our higher self and with the subtle worlds.

However, scientists have been steadily developing ever more sensitive instruments and methods that are slowly peeling back the layers between the world of our five senses and the higher frequency extrasensory worlds. It is quite likely that they will succeed in proving the reality of the etheric realm well before the public is ready to fully accept it, since it usually takes a long time to change entrenched cultural mind-sets.

If we look into the records of all world cultures, we can find stories, records and teachings about angels or devas within their lore, their religions and their ancient books of wisdom. *Deva* is a Sanskrit word that means "shining one" or "being of luminous light." In different cultures, these beings are known by other names, such as *malā'ikah* in the Qur'an and Hadith, *angelus* in Late Latin and *bird-people* to some North American aboriginals. In the western world today, they are most commonly known as *angels*—although some writers, such as David Spangler, classify angels as that branch of the deva kingdom that is more closely involved with human activities, such as religion, healing,

music and the arts.

In Zoroastrianism angelology, they are described as being responsible for manifesting God's energy. To the Jewish philosopher Maimonides, they are "the principles by which the physical universe operates" while, according to the Kabbalah, angels are considered to be an extension of God to produce effects in this world.

Esoteric teachings, both east and west, explain that our world consists of two parallel streams of evolution. Devas and humans each stand at the apex of a different life stream. These teachings recognize devas as a great evolution of intelligences that are engaged with all the forces, energies and patterns of matter within the universe. It cannot be just by chance that all major esoteric teachings and all major world religions recognize and respect these beings and honor them for the important role they play in creation.

The Realms of Manifestation

Although we know surprisingly little about them, the reality is that the manifestation of matter and form in our world—rock, plant, fish, animal, et cetera—would not be possible without the presence and activities of these remarkable intelligences. They are in charge of the evolution of matter and form. Or, as they explained to Dorothy Maclean: *Everything manifest is in our care, and we know its state, for under God we make plain His creation.*

Devas exist within a higher-frequency realm of energies that are a subtle yet intimate part of our world. They are formless intelligences that are limitless and free. They work with joy, wielding the forces and energies of creation, pursuing their vital activities in accordance with divine plan. All the patterns of forms that emanate from the Creator are passed down through many cosmic "levels" through the agency of ranks of devas working on each level to bring them ever further into physical manifestation.

In the vegetable kingdom, every form of plant life has a deva attending it. For example, tree devas are those intelligences involved with the trees of our world. Each tree species is overlighted by its own particular deva that is responsible for it, wherever it exists upon the earth.

A tree deva holds the energy pattern of its particular species and directs to each and every tree of that species the energies and forces necessary for its existence and continued well-being.

There is another division of the deva kingdom that works under the direction of these overlighting devas. They are the builder class— sometimes called "form-builder devas" or simply "builder devas." They pursue their busy life activities under the guidance of the greater devas, within a lower-frequency etheric realm. They work in groups to "materialize" the energy patterns of individual plants, minerals, water and all other physical forms that are part of the world of nature.

Many of these little form-builders are the "nature spirits" that were commonly known by such names as elves, fairies, water sprites, undines and others. They can be found in the folklore of most countries for, in earlier days, people lived closer to nature and were more aware of them and occasionally able to observe them. In our day and age, it is more often children who are unprejudiced enough and open enough to see these subtle workers. Our cultural beliefs and disbeliefs have helped to shutter our eyes to them for, just as "seeing is believing," in like fashion "believing is seeing."

This human tendency was pointed out to Dorothy Maclean by a deva:

If whatever exists is not "seen" in the minds of humans, in a sense it does not exist to humanity, but when humans recognize some new principle or energy or thing, then it is heaven brought down to earth; it becomes a reality to you.

Let us look at this process of manifestation in view of these two divisions of the deva realm, using trees for our example. Each species of tree has a species soul (a deva) that holds in its consciousness that tree's blueprint and directs to each tree of that species the required pattern of forces and energies that enables it to manifest in its characteristic species form. Under the guidance of this tree deva, groups of builder-devas (nature spirits) use the provided pattern to build its form or to "clothe" it in physical substance or planetary atomic matter so as to materialize the tree in its earthly body. It is a process that takes time and includes the familiar stages of physical growth that all things must go through from seed to maturity. The builders or nature spirits stay involved throughout all stages of the tree's growth and life, guided by its archetypal pattern existing in the ethers.

The entire process of manifestation unfolds within many different frequency levels as the idea originating from the Creator is passed on down through ranks of devas, from great archangels to a particular tree deva and finally to the realm of the form-builders, where it is built into its physical form—a process quite beyond human concepts and language.

One day, after admiring the beauty of an apple tree in full blossom, Dorothy decided to attune to the deva of that tree. During their exchange, the apple tree deva tried to paint a picture of this cosmic process of manifestation for her:

As from a seed a tree grows, so from a seed idea a pattern of force issues forth from the Creator, passed on by silent ranks of angels, silent and still because that idea is still too unformed and unfixed to endure any but the most exacting care. Down and out it comes, growing in strength and size, becoming brighter in pattern until eventually it scintillates and sounds, still in the care of the outmost angel. Its force field is steady and brilliant.

Then the force field is passed on to the makers of form to clothe that pattern. Remember this is a process—the pattern is everywhere apparent in the ethers, held by the angels and made manifest beyond time through the ministrations of the form workers at the appropriate opportunity—then appearing eventually in the beauty of the blossom and succulence of the fruit.

This is "the word made flesh." This is all Creation, held in balance by great layers of life of which your conscious mind is unaware. A miracle? You need a greater word.

The Nature of Nature Spirits

Over the years there have been many glamorized depictions of angels, fairies and elves, as well as many fanciful and romanticized ideas and stories written about them. However, some of the images and stories

published over the years have their roots in real contacts—primarily those made in earlier times. But these also carried their distortions. Today, fairies and angels have become popular once again and a great many stories, lore and imagery with all the same glamour can be found in every media. It is not surprising that most people choose to disbelieve their existence. This also creates problems for those individuals today who do have genuine contacts.

It must be understood that devas and nature spirits are part of a world of higher-frequency energies than ours. Devas exist in such subtle realms that they are rarely seen except by individuals with very highly attuned senses. But many more people can sense the presence of devas,

many can be inspired by them and some can establish contact with them in attuned states, as did Dorothy.

By contrast, nature spirits (form-builder devas) are occasionally seen by people, since they exist in the "etheric realm"—a subtle world that is of a denser frequency than that of the overlighting devas and one that lies just outside the reach of the senses of most individuals today. Although called a "realm," the etheric frequency is everywhere and is part of everything in existence. It is a subtle frequency level that science is just beginning to touch into. The human etheric body is often referred to as the vital body or human energy field—a subtle body that contains the seven energy centers commonly called chakras.

The etheric realm has different levels of density or frequency within it. The builder devas pursue their activities within its denser levels, where forms are still malleable—a subtle realm that acts as a gateway between the inner, formative worlds of the overlighting devas and the outer world of dense physical forms.

The etheric bodies of these little builder devas or nature spirits are vortices of dancing energy that are not visible to most human eyes today. They are sensitive to human energies and will usually flee when people are around. However, with sensitive people who are peaceful and close to nature, they sometimes make exceptions. If a nature spirit realizes such a person is able to see it and chooses not to flee, it will often veil itself in a human-like form in order to adopt an appearance more acceptable to the observer. Since they are aware of the thought-forms we hold of them, they will usually choose appearances to match those we expect to see. Nature spirits are not bound by gravity as are we, and this may cause a human observer to get the impression that some of them are flying as they busily move into and about the plants, pursuing their activities. This has led observers to believe they must be winged and has caused these nature spirits to respond by adapting an appearance with wings.

In earlier times, those farmers who were sensitive to nature and aware of the presence of nature spirits made a practice of setting aside a small part of their land as a woodlot—sometimes referred to as "God's little acre." As well as using the woodlot as a source of firewood, nuts, berries and other commodities, these farmers would retain a portion of the lot as an untouched wild area, out-of-bounds to humans. The purpose of this wild sanctuary was to provide a place of refuge not only for wildlife, but also for nature spirits attending to the local plant life. For these little builder devas not only act to materialize plants, but also work to help maintain them throughout their life cycles.

It should be mentioned that devas, angels and nature spirits are not the only beings found in the subtle realms. The non-physical dimensions of our world are vast realms teeming with countless forms of intelligent life, although unseen and almost unknown to us in these modern times. The names used in this book for those nature spirits that I call *elves* and *fairies* are based on what they are commonly called today. But there are other beings in the subtle worlds, quite different from them and of higher development, that are also referred to by these same names in some circles. I can say little more about this because it lies outside my knowledge and outside the scope of this book.

Modern Times

"Nature deficit disorder" is a recently identified syndrome caused by a lack of access to the natural world. Although it has not yet become an official medical diagnosis, it is definitely a common condition. More and more of our populations today are living in human-created, artificial urban worlds, and recently, some even in "virtual worlds." This is further distancing large numbers from the natural world and from the basic wisdom of our ancestors, who lived their lives more integrated with nature.

It is not that we should return to an earlier way of life, for that is neither wise nor possible; rather, we need to incorporate our ancestors' earthy wisdom and common-sense understanding of the natural world into the daily life of our modern culture.

Although our new technology offers definite advantages, it must be used with understanding and respect for the natural world, so that we become partners with nature rather than its controllers or abusers. This is the missing factor in most of our modern, mechanized, massive-scale, mono-cropping, genetically-altering, factory-farming, pesticide-and-herbicide-spreading farming and forestry practices. They are approaches that ignore the vital life needs of the waters, the soil, the plants and the creatures of nature that are deeply affected by them—approaches that don't recognize and respect them as kindred forms of life.

Most people would be surprised to learn that there would be no life on this planet without the activities of devas. Plants, for example, simply would not germinate and grow without their involvement. Since everything we plant does grow, regardless of the method used, how are devas affected by our manipulation of nature using these modern practices that don't respect the natural world? This question also concerned Dorothy Maclean and caused her to raise the issue with one of the devas. Here is the response she received:

As the rain falls on the just and unjust, we help to produce food for the good and the bad; the moral side of things is not our concern. We merely follow our destinies. We are man's friend or enemy depending on man himself. Our life is for the good; but man is making a mishmash of all life forces. On our level we are stable and man does not affect us, but on the level where he is, he can and he has affected us, and we cannot answer for the consequences. Should we not cooperate and build a new relationship?

Has our continual degradation of earth's ecosystems affected our biosphere? There is worldwide concern today about "climate change," and the reality of this change is becoming increasingly evident with each passing year in the form of extreme weather patterns everywhere. Yet most people don't seem to be making a clear connection between these changes and our ongoing destructive treatment of the forests and waters of our planetary home.

In one of Dorothy's inner exchanges on the topic of "oneness," the discussion turned to the issue of future climatic problems:

We would emphasize the practical side of oneness, the fact the bodies of all of you are one with the environment, and that you cannot abuse the environment of the earth without harming yourselves. No, it is not a new message, but humans don't seem to realize that oneness is not just on the high or inner levels where you place God. Oneness is right here and now. Disturbing the patterns of the earth, the balance of the seasons and the interplay of all aspects of matter, is cutting through the ordained out-working of this oneness and ruining prospects for the future of human kind.

Do you wonder at the violence of the elements? They will become much more violent unless humans pick up and act on this message.

It is interesting to note that this message is dated October 6, 1969.

* * *

REGREENING THE PLANET

In this age of reckless destruction of the environment, we are not without encouraging signs of change for the better. One such sign is the increasing number of people and organizations from all walks of life who are becoming more actively involved in efforts to restore the environment – and a great many of them are choosing to plant trees. Yet another sign of this same spirit is found in the increasing number of grassroots tree planting organizations springing up in every country.

A testament to the widespread public desire for restoring our ailing environment can be seen in the many environmental NGOs that have emerged from the private sector during the 1960s and ever since. These ENGOs, or "environmental non-governmental organizations," are not-for-profit groups started by people who felt they could no longer wait for governments to act, for if they did it would be too late to protect the many endangered ecosystems or to achieve sufficient public awareness to catalyze change.

Rise of the NGOs

In the last forty years, the number of environmental NGOs has increased significantly, ranging from larger, well-known organizations to smaller, locally supported groups. More recently, many have increased their focus on tree planting and forest preservation activities, reflecting the growing awareness of the urgent need to regreen the planet. An added blessing of these NGOs is that they offer ways for the average person to support environmental causes and, in some cases, to get directly involved with projects in nature.

These environmental organizations have developed a number of different strategies for accomplishing their objectives. It is impossible to list all the dedicated and inspired organizations that are doing such amazing work throughout the world today. Furthermore, I am not suggesting that those listed here are the best. What I am including here are examples of some of the different types of environmental NGO**s,** as well as examples of their most commonly used strategies.

Nature Conservancy, headquartered in Arlington, Virginia, is one of the world's first ENGOs and considered the world's leading conservation one. Its mission statement is simple and to-the-point: "to conserve the lands and waters on which all life depends."

In 1917, an activist wing of the U.S. Ecological Society published a catalog attempting to list all known wilderness patches remaining in North and Central America. In 1946, a small group of these scientists who desired to become more proactive formed the "Ecologists Union," resolving to help save threatened natural areas. It later changed its name to Nature Conservancy, and in 1951 incorporated as a non-profit organization.

Land acquisition is a key protection tool used by the conservancy, particularly in North America. They usually partner with local individuals or organizations to help purchase properties that are important ecosystems, using such instruments as land trusts and conservation easements. They then help set up local groups to protect and manage the properties. The conservancy provides financial help using their revolving "land preservation fund" that requires the loan be repaid for use in other conservation efforts. It has been highly successful with this approach and has an amazing record of accomplishments. Working in 69 countries, with over one million members, the Nature Conservancy today has protected more than 120 million acres of land, thousands of miles of rivers, and manages more than a hundred marine conservation projects globally.

World Wildlife Fund for Nature (WWF) was founded to remedy the desperate shortage of funds experienced by conservation groups. Sixteen of the world's leading conservationists, including the well-known biologist Sir Julian Huxley, signed the "Morges Manifesto" in 1961, calling for broad-based financial support. This led to the establishment of the World Wildlife Fund as a credible, international fund-raising organization for bringing substantial financial support to existing conservation efforts worldwide.

Today, WWF is the world's largest conservation organization, with over five million supporters. It is active in more than a hundred countries, supporting approximately 1,300 conservation and environmental projects.

Much of its focus is on protecting habitat of threatened species and establishing parks and nature reserves. In its website, WWF states: "… we are losing huge swathes of forests at an alarming rate. By 2020, we must conserve the world's forests to sustain nature's diversity, benefit our climate and support human well-being."

Leonardo DiCaprio Foundation (LDF), founded in 1998, is an example of the many NGOs started by well-known public figures. In one project, it has been working with other NGOs since 2010 to protect an endangered block of tropical forest in central Sumatra called

Bukit Tigapuluh or Thirty Hills. In 2015, they obtained a license to manage this 100,000-acre forest earmarked for logging, which borders the 330,000-acre Bukit Tigapuluh National Park, one of the last refuges in the region for critically endangered Sumatran tigers, elephants and orangutans. For Indonesia has lost almost half of its forests to pulp and palm oil plantations in just thirty years and has become one of the world's largest emitters of greenhouse gases.

The Thirty Hills project is a good example of the approach favored by most NGOs today when faced with large conservation projects—that of joining with other NGOs and working cooperatively with all local stakeholders to find mutually acceptable solutions. In this project, LDF together with WWF, FZS (Frankfurt Zoological Society) and TOP (The Orangutan Project) joined forces with local governments and communities to begin restoring the logged forest, as well as to maintain sufficient treed corridors to provide wildlife connections to other forest

blocks.

Earth Day Network is the largest NGO program in the world working to raise public awareness and to build a global environmental movement. The organization grew out of the first "Earth Day," on April 22, 1970, when it activated twenty million Americans and helped launch the modern environmental movement. Today it is working with more than 50,000 partners in 196 countries. More than one billion people now participate in Earth Day activities each year, making it the largest civic observance in the world.

Among its many environmental activities are regreening projects that include the Canopy Project, which has planted hundreds of millions of trees since 2010 in 32 countries in need of reforestation; and their recent and quite ambitious Trees For The Earth project, with its goal of planting 7.8 billion trees in deforested regions—one for each person on the planet—by Earth Day 2020.

It is commonly thought that the first Earth Day event was led mainly by environmental activists. But according to its president, Kathleen Rogers, many of the first organizers were blue-collar workers, housewives, teachers and other such people who had never before participated politically, but felt a call to help restore the environment.

Ancient Forest Alliance (AFA) was founded in 2010 by four dedicated environmental activists. It is an example of those NGOs created to help preserve specific ecosystems—in this case, the remaining ancient coastal forests of southern British Columbia. These native forests are an important part of First Nations' culture and home to Canada's largest and oldest trees, as well as some of Earth's last temperate rainforest wilderness. Nearly 25 percent of the world's temperate rainforest is in BC and most of it lies in coastal areas. Some of these hold immense ancient trees, such as Western red cedars up to five meters in diameter and over one thousand years old.

In December 2009, T.J. Watt, one of the founders of AFA, discovered a 50 hectare (123 acre) stand of ancient forest near Port Renfrew. It held huge Douglas firs and giant red cedars, including one with a massive twelve-foot diameter burl that has become known as "Canada's Gnarliest

Tree." This was a rare discovery, since 90 percent of the island's high-productivity old-growth forests have been logged—those like Avatar Grove, where the largest, monumental trees grow. What was surprising about this discovery was the grove's location, for it is situated close to Port Renfrew and easily accessible by good roads. But Watt also discovered that the grove's ancient trees were marked for cutting.

The Ancient Forest Alliance quickly launched a public campaign to preserve the area, naming it "Avatar Grove" after the lush forest world in the popular film *Avatar*. Due to their campaign, news of the grove quickly spread and began drawing large crowds of visitors from near and far. This awakened local governments to its potential for tourism and soon they and the public were calling for its protection. The AFA played a key role in raising public interest by providing news and maps and by building boardwalk hiking trails. After a brief but intense campaign, bolstered by strong public pressure, the AFA persuaded the BC government to set the grove aside from logging.

Ken Wu, co-founder of the AFA, says it has now become the second Cathedral Grove of British Columbia. "It's one of the finest groves of old growth in BC and it is generating hundreds of thousands of dollars for the local economy each year."

Approximately 80 percent of the productive forest lands of BC's southern coasts have been logged. Disappearing with them are vast numbers of plant and animal species that can thrive only in these diverse, old-growth ecosystems. Gone too are many sources of clean water and streams with their spawning sites for salmon. And, as the AFA points out in their website, these ancient forests are "fundamental pillars of BC's multi-billion-dollar tourism industry."

This last point is an interesting one. "Super, Natural British Columbia" is a registered trademark of BC and the province's tourism brand. Their destinationbc.ca website explains its meaning as follows: "We are a province shaped by nature. BC, like its people and its visitors, is 'wild at heart'." Unfortunately, these same sentiments are not reflected in BC's long-standing destructive forestry policies. It must be clear by now that an old-growth forest's timber value is short-lived, while its tourism value in today's world will only keep growing for many generations.

The Unstoppable Wangari Maathai

It was among the native people of Kenya, in 1920, that St. Barbe Baker was able to organize the "Watuwa Miti," the first volunteer movement for planting trees and protecting forests, that later evolved into the international Men of the Trees organization. It was also in Kenya where, in 1977, an important environmental figure emerged and established another famous tree-planting organization known as the Green Belt Movement.

Wangari Maathai (1940 – 2011), the internationally renowned environmental political activist, was born in Nyeri, a rural agricultural area of Kenya. She was an exceptional individual who worked tirelessly on many levels to light fires of inspiration, to challenge political corruption and to create practical solutions for tackling environmental and social problems.

The young Kikuyu girl grew up in the early 1940s in the lush, central highlands of Kenya. There, she tells us, people enjoyed clean waters, rich soil, thick forests with leopards and elephants, and there was work for everyone.

"It was heaven. We wanted for nothing," she said. "Now the forests have come down, the land has been turned to commercial farming, the tea plantations keep everyone poor, and the economic system does not allow people to appreciate the beauty of where they live."

A bright student, Wangari Maathai became one of the first 300 Kenyans selected to study in the United States in 1960 under the "Airlift Africa" educational program funded by John F. Kennedy. She obtained a degree in biological sciences from Mount St. Scholastica College in Kansas and then a master of science degree from the University of Pittsburgh. After pursuing doctoral studies in Germany, she entered the University of Nairobi and in 1971 became the first East African woman to obtain a PhD. She later joined the university's faculty and in 1976 became the first woman in the region to chair a university department.

Through her work with various volunteer associations, it became evident to Mathai that the root cause of most of Kenya's problems was environmental degradation of their forests and land caused by "development." In 1976, while serving in the National Council of Women, she introduced the idea of community-based tree planting. She continued to develop this idea and eventually established the Green Belt Movement (GBM), a broad-based grassroots organization whose main focus is environmental conservation and poverty reduction through tree planting. It organizes women in rural Kenya to plant trees, combat deforestation and stop soil erosion in order to restore their main source of fuel for cooking and to generate income. "Women needed income and they needed resources because theirs were being depleted," she explained to *People* magazine. "So we decided to solve both problems together."

She encouraged the women of Kenya to plant tree nurseries throughout the country and to search nearby forests to obtain the seeds for this so that they would propagate trees native to the area. She agreed to pay the women a small stipend for each seedling that was later planted elsewhere.

In 1974 Wangari Maathai was asked to join the local board of the Environment Liaison Centre and eventually became board chair. The centre works to promote the participation of nongovernmental organizations in the work of the United Nations Environmental Program (UNEP), whose headquarters in Africa later became established in Nairobi, Kenya, in 1996.

At the UN's third global women's conference she made presentations and gained wider attention for the work of the Green Belt Movement. Her efforts attracted the interest of other African countries that were seeking ways to combat the growing problems of desertification, deforestation, water crisis and rural hunger. In 1986, with funding from UNEP, the movement spread throughout Africa and led to founding the Pan-African Green Belt Network in fifteen African countries. The attention the movement received in the media led to Professor Mathai being honored with many international awards.

In 1989, after various unsuccessful efforts to prevent the construction of a skyscraper in Uhuru Park, including a court injunction, Wangari Maathai and her GBM group staged a protest in the park. As she explained to several international papers, the proposed project would be the equivalent of building a skyscraper in Hyde Park or Central Park. Her campaign drew such public support and international attention that the government finally dropped the project.

She also kept challenging Kenya's governments on its undemocratic development plans and its handling of the country's environment. She organized protests and was an outspoken critic of dictator Daniel arap Moi while he was in power. This led to her being beaten and arrested numerous times. Eventually the green belt environmental movement became a political effort as well.

"Nobody would have bothered with me if all I did was to encourage women to plant trees." she told *The Economist*. "But I started seeing the linkages between the problems that we were dealing with and the root causes of environmental degradation. And one of those root causes was misgovernance."

In the early 1990s, Maathai set up Mazingira, the Kenyan Green Party, and won 98 percent of the votes in her constituency. She then joined a coalition that finally overthrew Moi in 2002. She served as assistant environment minister in the government until November

2005.

By 2005, the Green Belt Movement had grown from being a few women planting trees to a network of 600 community groups caring for 6,000 tree nurseries that were often run by disabled and mentally challenged villagers. The movement has branches in thirty counties.

Wangari Maathai was awarded the Nobel Peace Prize in 2004. In its citation the Norwegian Nobel Committee stated that she "stands at the front of the fight to promote ecologically viable social, economic and cultural development in Kenya and in Africa. She thinks globally and acts locally." In accepting the award, Professor Maathai said, "I always felt that our work was not simply about planting trees. It was about inspiring people to take charge of their environment, the system that governed them, their lives, and their future."

By 2014 the Green Belt Movement had planted over 51 million trees and trained over 30,000 women in forestry, food processing, bee-keeping and other trades, while preserving their lands and resources. Communities in Kenya (men and women) have been motivated and organized to restore their damaged environment and to prevent any further destruction to it.

Wangari Maathai has influenced many people and organizations internationally. Throughout her life, she consistently inspired others by her speeches, her writings and her actions. She always stressed the importance of communities taking responsibility for their local needs. "It's the little things citizens do; that's what will make the difference." Says Wangari, "My little thing is planting trees."

In *Replenishing the Earth: Spiritual Values for Healing Ourselves and the World*, one of her four published books, she reflects:

"We can appreciate the delicacy of dew or a flower in bloom, water as it runs over pebbles, the majesty of an elephant or leaves blowing in the wind. Such aesthetic responses are valid in their own right, and as reactions to the natural world they can inspire in us a sense of wonder and beauty that in turn encourages a sense of the divine. That consciousness acknowledges that while a certain tree, forest, or mountain itself may not be holy, the life-sustaining services it provides—the oxygen we breathe, the water we drink—are what make existence possible, and so deserve our respect and veneration. From

this point of view the environment becomes sacred, because to destroy what is essential to life is to destroy life itself."

* * *

There are trees for almost all human needs.
One of the greatest teachers of India was the Buddha,
who included in his teaching the obligation of every good
Buddhist that he should plant and see to the establishment of
one tree at least every five years. As long as this was observed, the
whole large area of India was covered with trees, free of dust,
with plenty of water, plenty of shade, plenty of food and materials.
Just imagine you could establish an ideology which made it
obligatory for every able-bodied person in India,
man, woman and child, to do that little thing—to plant
and see to the establishment of one tree a year, five years
running. This, in a five-year period, would give you 2,000
million established trees. Anyone can work it out on the back of
an envelope that the economic value of such
an enterprise, intelligently conducted, would be greater than
anything that has ever been promised by any of India's five-year
plans. It could be done without a penny of foreign aid; there
is no problem of savings and investments. It would produce
foodstuffs, fibers, building materials, shade,
water, almost anything that man really needs.

E.F. Schumacher
Small is Beautiful, A Study of Economics as if People Mattered,
1973, HarperCollins Publisher

THE
TRILLION
TREE KID

The Billion Tree Campaign was launched in 2006 by the United Nations Environment Program (UNEP) as a response to the challenges of global warming and a wide array of other sustainability challenges that ranged from water supply to biodiversity loss. UNEP is the UN's voice for environmental matters. Under UNEP's leadership and through proactive advocacy by patrons and partners, the campaign catalyzed tree planting action on all continents. The response to the program was unexpectedly strong and widespread, causing it to grow into one of the largest regreening campaigns to date. UNEP's campaign was similar to an NGO campaign, in that it relied on volunteer individuals, companies and governments to finance and accomplish its goals.

The Billion Tree Campaign was effective in catalyzing tree planting on every continent. The billionth tree, an African olive, was planted in Ethiopia in 2007. After this speedy fulfillment of its goal, the campaign set its next target of 7 billion planted trees by the time of the 2009 Climate Change conference in Denmark. Again, the response was so great it was completed three months early. A "Twitter for Trees" campaign was added in 2009 that proved to be very effective and helped to mobilize tree planting action across the globe for the next two years, until UNEP decided to end its involvement in the program.

"Looking back over the Billion Tree Campaign, what is most remarkable is not its scale, but its spread," said UNEP executive director Achim Steiner. "People from all around the world enthusiastically joined the campaign and planted trees in their own communities."

The inspiration for UNEP's Billion Tree Campaign had come from a statement made by Wangari Maathai. One day, while she was at UNEP's African headquarters in Nairobi, Kenya, an American executive told her that his corporation planned to plant a million trees. "That's great," she replied, "but what we really need is to plant a billion trees."

In 2011, UNEP handed over its successful tree-planting project to the Plant-for-the-Planet Foundation, which had been actively participating since 2007. By that time, the campaign had registered over 12.5 billion planted trees in 193 countries.

You might wonder why UNEP would hand over such a large international campaign to a children's organization headed by a thirteen-year-old kid. On the face of it, their decision certainly seems questionable—but not if you know its inspired leader, Felix Finkbeiner.

Plant-for-the-Planet is a children's initiative that was initially based in Tutzing, Bavaria. Its goal is to raise awareness about climate change and global justice using the planting of trees as a practical and symbolic action. The idea was the inspiration of a nine-year-old German boy named Felix Finkbeiner. While doing research for a school report on climate change, Felix came across a story about the dedicated environmentalist Wangari Maathai and her Green Belt Movement that had planted 30 million trees, and he became greatly moved and motivated by it.

After presenting his climate change report at school, Felix used the occasion to propose a vision he had—that the children of the world plant one million trees in every country on Earth. His speech was so compelling that his inspiration gained the support of his school to put it into action. In 2007 he planted the first tree at the school and officially launched Plant-for-the-Planet. He continued giving his talk at other schools and soon students from across Germany became involved in tree planting under the initiative's name. One of the older students created a website and Felix and his friends set up a competition with other German schools to see which could plant the most trees. This gave a boost to the momentum of the initiative and to the number of trees planted. It also gave a boost to the number of calls from other students wanting to join Plant-For-The-Planet. The group was now becoming very busy and he decided they needed to hire a full-time employee.

To obtain the needed funds, Felix decided to call Toyota, a major car company with green credentials, to ask them for 40,000 Euros to hire a full-time staff member. Surprisingly, Toyota agreed. Later, when he gave his talk at the local rotary club, the CEO of Toyota Germany, Lothar Feuser, was in the audience—possibly to size up Felix and their investment. So impressed was he with Felix that he invited him to the next annual gathering of German Toyota Dealers, where the boy again delivered his message. The dealers attending the meeting found his speech so compelling, they spontaneously pledged 11,000 Euros in donations to Plant-For-The Planet. It also inspired them to begin tree-planting projects in their local areas.

In April 2008, ten-year-old Felix called a press conference and announced to a packed gathering that they had planted 50,000 trees. Later that year he addressed the European Parliament and, in the same year, was elected to the UNEP Children's Board. He was chosen by the board to speak at the UNEP Tunza Children and Youth Conference in South Korea in 2009. Once again, he was able to inspire the gathering and succeeded in gaining their support for Plant-for-the-Planet from children around the world, who promised to plant a million trees in their own countries.

Plant-for-the-Planet then became an international NGO, supported by the United Nations, and initiated a global campaign entitled "Stop talking. Start planting" to suggest that, while adults are talking about climate change, children are doing something about it.

Felix Finkbeiner was now well under way toward achieving his initial vision. But he is not just a visionary; he has proved to be a practical and effective planner with organizational skills. To ensure that the registered trees are valid and planted correctly, tree planters are required to find foresters or environmental organizations to supply native species of seedlings and to supervise planting. There is also a system of independent auditors to guarantee the number of trees planted.

An important part of the foundation's work are the well-organized, international programs that train children, between ages nine to twelve, to become Ambassadors for Climate Justice. Ambassadors are taught about the climate crisis and learn how to prepare and present these ideas to other children in a confident and interesting way at educational gatherings called "academies."

It is rare for a child to be invited to speak to the UN General Assembly, but in 2011 thirteen-year-old Felix spoke to open the United Nation's International Year of Forests. "We children know adults know the challenges and they know the solutions," he told the UN delegation. "But we don't know why there is so little action." Felix then suggested three possible reasons:

The first is simply denial. A second is that many adults act like monkeys: "If you let a monkey choose if he wants one banana now or six bananas later, he always chooses the one banana now." A third is differing perspectives: "For adults it is an academic question if sea levels rise three centimeters or seven meters by the end of this century. But for us children it is a question of survival."

Finkbeiner is a gifted orator and, as is evident, he is not afraid to speak his mind. He is determined that children should have a voice in environmental matters. As he explains; "We children have understood we cannot trust that adults alone will save our future. We have to take our future into our own hands."

Change Chocolate

Seeking for a way to help finance operations, Felix turned to chocolate. In 2011, the 13-year-old Felix spoke at a meeting of 350 international chocolate producers to seek their help. He pointed out to the assembly that kids were major chocolate customers, and proposed the industry donate 0.01 percent of sales or one euro per ton of chocolate to Plant-for-the-Planet. He suggested it be called a "Future Fee." After completing his proposal, Felix waited for feedback. But there was absolutely no response from the producers. Surprised and dismayed by the silence, Felix uttered, "This is shocking," and left the stage in tears.

Angry, but quite unwilling to give up, Felix and Plant-for-the-Planet launched their own chocolate product operation in 2012 called Change Chocolate—a fair-trade-certified, climate-neutral product that pays fair wages. It quickly developed into the best-selling fair-trade chocolate company in Germany and Austria. For every bar sold, 20 cents goes towards planting trees, while 10 cents goes towards training more ambassadors. By January 30, 2017, Change Chocolate had sold 9 million bars of chocolate and enabled more than 2 million trees to be planted.

A Giant Leap of Faith

After taking over UNEP's Billion Tree Campaign in 2011, Plant-for-the-Planet declared their next goals are to plant one trillion trees (1,000 billion) worldwide by 2020 and to motivate a million children to become Climate Justice Ambassadors to expand their global network. (There are currently 63,000 ambassadors active in 58 countries and over 100,000 children worldwide organised in planting trees.) Since they were quite aware that it took five years for the UNEP program to achieve 15.5 billion planted trees, the proposal to plant 65 times that number in nine years was quite an ambitious target. But Felix thinks globally and acts globally and is not one to be daunted by numbers. He also has his reasons for choosing the goal of a trillion planted trees.

"We had scientists work out the maximum number of trees that can be planted without encroaching on land that's needed for agricultural purposes," he explained, "They told us it was around a trillion, so that's the goal we've set to maximize the ability of trees to sequester CO_2. A trillion trees could take in one-quarter of the CO_2 humans pump out every year, helping keep temperature rise within the critical 2-degree limit, not to mention clean the air, balance water cycles and water tables and provide a living for millions of people."

Many of the trillion trees will be planted in the warm global south, where trees grow fast and are less costly to both plant and maintain—as little as ten cents a tree according to the Trillion Tree Campaign website. This is probably one of the reasons why his foundation chose to purchase the 13,500 hectare (33,359 acre) deforested land in Campeche province, near Cancun, Mexico, in 2014. Felix is immensely proud of the new Plant-for-the-Planet Ranch that now employs 78 people in an effort to plant 10 million trees on the land by 2020.

When questioned about the feasibility of planting a trillion trees, Finkbeiner points out that the initiative's timing is good. One-quarter of all the emissions reductions pledged by countries in the 2015 Paris agreement will come from tree planting and land restoration. Many countries, including the UK, US and Germany, have pledged to plant and restore large areas of land, many of which are degraded forests. The UN has set a target of restoring 350 million hectares of forest (865 million acres) by 2030—an area larger than India. China plans to create new forests the size of Ireland, and a number of Latin American countries have promised large-scale reforestation. Most African countries, on the other hand, are strongly focused on agroforestry, along with projects to restore degraded forests.

Twenty-year-old Felix is currently studying international relations at the University of London. He is keeping his options for the future open, while looking for the best way to achieve his primary goal—to join in the effort to solve global problems. We can expect to hear more about this young man in the near future.

The remarkable vitality, vision and success of Felix Finkbeiner and the international youth organization that he has created, its global vision and willingness to take on ever-larger volunteer projects to restore the environment, is a most hopeful sign for our future.

***

The climate crisis does not need technological intervention to resolve it, because trees are by far the simplest and most efficient way to absorb the world's emissions. Why not use them? Sometimes adults are really difficult to understand.

Felix Finkbeiner

FOREST CONSCIOUSNESS

There is a growing interest among the plant scientists of today to understand the nature and mechanisms of plant consciousness. In 2005, an international group of six scientists, comprised of plant biologists, plant physiologists and plant ecologists, proposed a new field of scientific inquiry to explore the sensory aspect of plant biology. They had recognized the need for a new field of study in order to better understand how plants are able to recognise and respond in such integrated ways to so many environmental variables, such as light, water, gravity, temperature, soil composition, microbes, toxins, attacks from various feeding creatures, and signals from other plants. They also noted that electrical and chemical signalling systems found in plants are similar to those found in animal nervous systems and also utilize similar neurotransmitters such as serotonin, dopamine and glutamate.

All these factors suggested to these scientists that plants possess a brain-like ability to process information, integrate the data and then develop appropriate behavioral responses. This pointed to the need for a new scientific field of "plant neurobiology," as they proposed to call it. Eventually, the groups' proposal led to the creation of a new scientific society, and a journal called *Plant Signaling and Behavior*, which they decided would be a less controversial title. Its purpose is to provide a cross-disciplinary forum for exploring and sharing the growing scientific information relating to the biological mechanisms of plant intelligence.

Recent research indicates that plants use their intelligence for more than just personal survival and, moreover, that they possess an ability to communicate and interact with other plants in cooperative and coordinated ways. From evidence emerging out of various scientific studies over the last 25 years, it is becoming increasingly clear that established forests are intelligent, integrated tree and plant communities that are able to meet their challenges by sharing information and then responding in appropriate ways as a group to deal with problems and to maintain stable conditions.

Forest Cooperation

In the 1990s, forestry scientist Dr. Suzanne Simard of the University of British Columbia was conducting research to determine why weeding

out birch trees from new plantations of Douglas firs would cause the fir trees to weaken and decline. When she uncovered the roots of these same species in an old-growth forest location, she discovered an extensive below-ground fungal network linking the roots of birches and firs with each other and with the soil. To find if it was this fungal system that held the answer to her research question, she conducted a series of microscopic experiments. Using radioactive carbon, Dr. Simard traced and measured the flow and sharing of carbon through this network between individual trees. This led her to discover that these complex mycelium webs allow trees to interact with one another by conducting exchanges of carbon, nutrients and water.

These findings offered an answer to the problem she was trying to solve, for they showed that the interspecies partnerships between birches and firs is a dynamic one and that both species were benefiting in exchanges of nutrients that fluctuated back and forth according to the season. Sometimes the fir trees received more of the nutrients while at other times it was the birches that were the main beneficiaries. It was evident that this system of exchanging nutrients particularly favored exchanges between deciduous and coniferous trees, since their energy deficits occur during different times of the year. The fungi that mediated this cooperative process also benefited from their part in these activities by receiving a share of the nutrients being exchanged.

Mycorrhizal fungi have existed since plants first appeared on dry land. These fine strands of filaments grow in networks and form close interdependent relationships with the roots of plants. The fungi make available nutrients they are able to draw from the soil that the roots of plants are not otherwise able to access. In return, the fungi receive carbohydrates and other nutrients that the plants manufacture. This long-standing symbiotic relationship greatly benefits the plants, enhancing their growth and stimulating the development of their roots.

Dr. Susan Simard's findings were published in *Nature* magazine in 1997, where the term "wood-wide web" was coined in reference to this underground mycelium network. Her research showed that these vast fungal systems, comprised of long, branching filamentous strands, were integral to the life of the remarkably fertile West Coast forests. It is now widely accepted by scientists that mycorrhizal systems are an integral part of forests and that they amplify the ability of all forest plants and trees to absorb water and nutrients and to resist pathogens. As Dr. Simard remarks: "The benefit of this cooperative underground economy appears to be better overall health, more total photosynthesis, and greater resilience in the face of disturbance."

Since her initial research, Dr. Simard and other researchers have established that all forest trees, regardless of species, make use of their interconnected root systems and fungal networks to share resources. Those trees that enjoy the most advantageous forest conditions and have a surplus of sugar share with those that are experiencing less favorable conditions and are in need.

Such discoveries show that forest trees act as a group to take good care of each other. And they demonstrate a caring nature that is surprisingly strong. In some mature forests one can occasionally find stumps of trees that were felled many years ago. These "trees knees," as they are called in British Columbia, have managed to grow a top covering and are solid, without decay and still quite alive—for these living stumps continue to be fed and supported through their roots by the surrounding forest community.

Mother Trees

Dr. Simard's research did not end with her discoveries about the relationship between trees and the "wood-wide web." As she continued with her studies she began to recognize and identify the various activities of what she termed "mother trees"—the older, larger trees of the forest that are key focal points in the connected activities taking place on the root and mycorrhizal networks. Moreover, she found that these big trees are important to the health of the whole forest. They act as central hubs within the tree/fungi complex and play a primary role in managing the resources of the entire plant community.

These are not the only reasons for referring to the big, older trees as mother trees, for as well as managing forest resources and providing the best possible source of seeds for their species, they perform other important maternal functions. Dr. Simard found that they assist their young by infecting them with fungi to help connect them into the forest mycorrhizal network for receiving nutrients and community support. Mother trees then use this fungal link for directly supplying their saplings with the food they need for growth.

Another discovery was that mother trees appear to be "family oriented." Douglas fir mother trees, for example, were found to be directing more carbon to their own baby firs than to unrelated, random baby firs. This of course implies that they are aware of which of the youngsters are their own offspring. More surprising, she found that when a baby tree happens to grow close to its mother tree, the latter will alter its root structures in order to make room for the young tree to grow. What is not surprising was Simard's finding that when mother trees are cut down, the survival rate of the forest's youngest trees are substantially diminished. In her words: "The big trees were subsidizing the young ones through fungal networks. Without this helping hand, most of the seedlings wouldn't make it."

It is hoped that these revelations will eventually influence the forest industry's approach to tree harvesting. For Dr. Simard's work and that of other scientists makes it evident that leaving some key mother trees standing in various locations would foster the renewal of a forest in a quicker and healthier way. It also highlights the necessity for conducting logging operations in a way that minimizes the disturbance of underground fungi systems. In soils that have been disturbed by human activity, the quantity of mycorrhizae can be so drastically decreased that there are not enough to produce a significant benefit to the growth and health of plants.

Forest Communication

The widespread network of roots and fungal filaments that link up forest trees enables a forest to function as a kind of integrated organism—a connected, interacting tree community. This underground "internet" provides a forest with a form of group consciousness that gives it an ability to respond in a unified way when dealing with environmental stresses. Scientists are still discovering the many ways in which forest trees are able to act in unison to deal with the challenges they face.

In his fascinating book *The Hidden Life of Trees: What They Feel,*

How They Communicate, the German forester Peter Wohlleben discusses the communal life of forest trees in considerable detail. Drawing upon scientific knowledge as well as personal observations made during his many years in his native German forests, he provides many remarkable insights into the inner life of trees. If you read his book you will have quite a different experience the next time you go for a walk in a woods.

Peter Wohlleben writes about the nature of the communications that occur between trees in forest communities. He refers to scientific studies showing that forest trees are in constant communication with each other. They accomplish this by two methods. One is by releasing scented aerosol "messages" from pores located in the underside of their leaves that disperse throughout forest airways and are received by their neighbors. The other method is made possible because the root systems of trees grow into one another. This enables them to convey messages to their neighbors by sending chemical signals through their roots. Alternately, according to recent findings, trees can also use their root connections to send messages to each other by transmitting electrical

impulses. In addition, as mentioned previously, trees make use of widespread underground fungal networks to extend the range of their messages much farther, enabling them to communicate with the broader forest community. This ability to exchange information with one another allows forest trees to coordinate their efforts in dealing with many kinds of problems.

When trees are under attack from insect predators or other such dangers, they are able to respond in a variety of ways to meet the challenge. If undergoing an insect infestation, they can alter their internal chemistry to produce compounds that make their tissues less palatable to the feeding pest. Alternately they may release specific aerosol scent signals from their leaves to attract those insect predators that like to feed on the species attacking them.

While taking these defensive actions, they will also send out warning of the new danger to their neighbors. Using chemical or electrical signals transmitted through their root and fungal networks, or aerosol scents released from their leaves, they send messages to alert neighboring trees.

And the information they send is remarkably specific, for it enables their neighbors to know the exact nature of the danger and allows them time to make appropriate preparations. It is quite possible that they may also convey the most effective method they have found for dealing with the problem. In this way, forest trees share information and join forces to reduce or prevent infestations and to deal with many other environmental challenges.

Forest Trees use Teamwork to Beat the Heat

The world-renowned scientist and environmentalist Dr. David Suzuki hosts a popular CBC television series, now in its 58th season, called *The Nature of Things*—a widely aired, science-based documentary program that frequently focuses on nature and the environment. These televised programs present leading-edge scientific discoveries and traditional aboriginal knowledge about these issues, sometimes utilizing animated illustrations to help make complex issues more understandable to the average viewer.

A recent program focused on scientific studies being carried out in Finland's boreal forest by atmospheric chemist Joel Thornton from the University of Washington. These studies, conducted in a highly sophisticated forest research station in Finland, have helped explain the method used by boreal trees to deal with periods of hot dry weather. Although forest trees can't hide from the heat, Thornton found that they have an effective way of dealing with it. Through his atmospheric research studies, he discovered that boreal conifers are able to act in unison to generate cloud cover when they need to beat the heat.

During stretches of hot, sunny weather, all boreal conifers simultaneously begin to release increased amounts of terpenes from their needles. Terpenes are organic compounds similar to the familiar, wonderfully scented compounds that one can smell around Christmas trees. These invisible terpene molecules rise into the atmosphere, where they meet and collide with ozone molecules and then combine with them to create larger particles. As more terpene molecules rise, they collide and join up with these larger particles, causing them to continue growing into ever-larger molecules. Once the molecules reach a certain size, water vapor begins to condense on their surface, in much the same way as steam from a bathroom shower will condense on a shower door. Eventually, as the water vapor molecules increase in number, they form a visible mist. Before long, the gathering mist grows into fluffy white clouds, providing the boreal trees with cooling shade and relief from the heat.

Once again we find that forest trees are able to influence weather patterns. And the weather conditions created by these northern conifers are not just local phenomena. The circumpolar boreal is a huge global area and the weather conditions generated by its trees affect wide areas of the northern hemisphere. They are important to its vast water systems that are so vital to the whole planet—for the boreal region that rings the crown of the planet is home to the largest freshwater reserves on earth.

* * *

OLD GROWTH GUARDIANS

An old-growth forest is a community of trees of mixed species in all stages of development, from seedlings to the larger and older mother trees. An established tree community creates its own preferred microclimate and attracts the right flora and fauna it requires to maintain a healthy and balanced state. The larger trees are key for providing the optimum conditions of shade, moisture, temperature and shelter from wind that an established forest requires, as well as the conditions needed to nurture and protect a healthy younger generation of trees. Even when the old trees die, their bodies continue to serve the forest—first as homes for many creatures such as woodpeckers, owls, and squirrels. Once they topple, their decaying trunks along with the yearly leaf litter and fallen branches are primary builders of healthy forest soils. These soils and the moist, shaded conditions created by big trees are essential for the bacteria, fungi, soil organisms, mosses, flowers, ferns, shrubs and tree seedlings that together form the rich carpet of life of a forest floor.

Animals, birds and insects are also an integral part of healthy forest ecosystems. For example, flying squirrels play a role in developing and maintaining the below-ground fungal networks that underlie a forest. These busy little creatures feed on the fruiting bodies of the fungi and then disperse their spores widely as they glide about the woods during their nightly activities.

In West Coast rain forests, bears provide a similar service. Analysis of core samples taken from old-growth trees there show that over 85 percent of their yearly nitrogen content comes from salmon. This important nutrient is delivered to the trees through the activities of bears. During the yearly salmon spawning runs up the West Coast inland rivers and streams, there, many bears migrate to these waterways to feed on the fish. It is an important event for the bears, as they need to build up fat reserves for the coming winter months. They catch salmon in great numbers and, in the process of feeding on them, scatter their remains throughout the woods. Then the omnipresent fungi assist the process by helping to digest the fish remains and to distribute them more widely throughout the forest.

Misconceptions

Certain beliefs that have become entrenched in forestry practice need to be reexamined. One such belief is that after 60 to 120 years, depending on the species, the growth energy of a tree slows down. Young trees, on the other hand, are believed to grow faster and therefore to be more productive in creating wood for harvesting, as well as being more effective for carbon sequestering. For this reason, it is considered good forestry practice to remove the older, larger trees and replace them with young trees in order to "rejuvenate" the forest.

Rejuvenate is certainly the right term to use for a practice of eradicating all the elders and replacing them with juveniles. Human civilizations would be a mess if we made "eldercide" a practice in human populations and left everything in the hands of juveniles.

Rather than restricting the development of young trees around them, the large, older trees protect and foster them. They play a key role in creating the optimal conditions of moisture and shade needed by the younger trees. Being appropriately shaded allows them to grow at a slower pace so as to develop smaller and tighter cell structures—a development that will provide them with the strength and resiliency they will need when it is their turn to become the tall, old-growth elders in the woods. "Slow-growth" trees may prove to be even more important in the future as weather conditions, such as strong winds, continue to become more extreme due to climate change. Because the trees in forest plantations grow in open clearcut areas, they grow faster than trees in mature forests and have larger, more open cell structures. For this reason, lumber derived from such trees is weaker than that derived from old-growth trees. Building codes recognise this difference and distinguish between the strength of the two.

In the 1980s I came across a government pamphlet that was issued as a guide for the management of private woodlots. It contained an illustration of a large tree surrounded by a forest of smaller trees. The artist somehow managed to make the big tree appear ugly and threatening. The caption under the illustration explained that the big tree was a "wolf tree" that was hogging all the light and preventing the younger trees from growing. The pamphlet recommended that property owners get rid of all such wolfish trees in order to create a healthier woodlot.

It is also believed that all trees compete for light and will do much better if competing neighbors are removed. This idea suggests that a tree's life is a struggle for survival in a ruthless world of competition. However, in his book *The Hidden Life of Trees*, Peter Wohllenben says that forests of beech trees in western Germany were discovered to be more productive when allowed to grow close together in their natural way. In fact, the annual increase in biomass proved that these natural forests were much healthier than those that were thinned. All the trees in natural beech forests fared well. It didn't matter which of the trees received more light, as they all shared resources among themselves via their interconnected root and mycelium networks. Rather than competing with each other, they cooperated as a group and those with abundance of sugar gave, while those in need received.

Another common misconception is that by removing mature trees and replacing them with sapling transplants, the fast-growing young trees will sequester more carbon than established elders and so be of greater value in the fight against global warming. But Peter Wohlleben reports the results of a study by an international team of scientists that refutes this idea that young trees are more productive. Their study, which examined approximately 700,000 trees on every continent, showed that trees having trunks three feet in diameter generated three times as much biomass as trees only half as wide. It is easy to understand the reason for this. Each year a tree adds a growth ring layer to its trunk. Hence a tree having a large diameter trunk will lay down a larger growth ring and create more biomass yearly than one having a smaller diameter trunk. This is why old-growth forests are estimated to store two or three times

more carbon per hectare per year than second-growth plantations.

This international study provides scientific proof that older trees are not slowing down because of age, but instead are even more active, full of vitality and highly productive. It also means they are more effective at sequestering carbon than are juvenile trees. If we want to use trees in the fight against climate change, it is evident that we would do far better to allow them to grow old.

The loss of old-growth forest trees is creating another serious problem—their eradication is increasingly reducing the level of genetic diversity within individual species. Any reduction of diversity within a species creates a reduction in its ability to adapt to stresses. Genetic diversity is a measure of the genetic variation between members of the same species. A high level of genetic diversity within a species gives it a greater chance of adapting to and surviving various challenges—including insect infestations like forest tent caterpillars, such diseases as the butternut canker, or even environmental changes like pollution and global warming.

When the older trees of a forest are lost, the forest's future is put at risk, for they are its prime seed trees—the trees that embody the greatest level of genetic diversity and hence are able to provide the highest quality seeds for the future of its species. At the very least, before an area is logged, it should be required that stands of prime, big trees be selected in various locations and left standing to ensure a healthy future for the forest. This is only common sense.

In her book *The Global Forest*, Diana Beresford-Kroeger offers an easy-to-follow method for those who wish to create a new woodlot or treed area. This approach suggests selecting transplants grown from seeds obtained from the oldest and healthiest native tree species to be found in the same locality. These transplants are then used as "epicenter trees," since they have the best genetic ability to hold their own through the potentially difficult periods of climate change ahead. They should be protected as needed from deer, rabbits and mice, until beyond all such dangers. Next, a mixture of native evergreen and deciduous trees should be planted among the epicenter trees to provide biodiversity—either by seedings or by sapling transplants, or both. To round out the work, native forest perennials from the same locality can be planted among the trees.

Before long, this newly created natural area will begin to attract birds and animals that, together with the wind, will begin to introduce other organisms and help generate a complex, new ecosystem.

Because forest trees have been classified as a "renewable resource," we are given the impression that it is almost environmentally correct to cut and replant them as if they were crops of corn. It is a classification that has helped promote wasteful and highly damaging systems of forest management worldwide—systems, such as clearcutting—that are designed to help the highly mechanized forest industry more easily cut our ancient forests with heavy equipment. They would argue, "What's the problem? We will replace the old trees with a new crop of the best market species. We will create a better forest that will grow faster, have a higher market value, and be more economical to harvest, since all the trees will be ready to cut at the same time."

The reality is that centuries-old forests are rich, biodiverse ecosystems teeming with life, while these tree plantations with their mono-age, mono-species crops and compacted soils are, in comparison, virtual "dead zones" with very few insects, birds, animals and other plants. Clear-cutting acres of native forests is a heartless practice that is killing far more than trees, for it is steadily eradicating countless forms of living things at the same time. We know it is possible to manage forests in a more balanced way so as to serve both Nature and human needs, for there are forested regions that have already adopted such approaches.

It is hard to believe, but according to statistics, our planet is currently losing over 50 acres of forest every minute. Therefore, if we wish to help protect the environment and combat climate change, one of the most effective actions almost every able-bodied person can take is to plant trees, since they are needed in vast numbers everywhere. Trees are great environmental healers and, given time and sufficient numbers, have the ability to do much to mend a wounded planet.

But the Problem is...

But the problem is—planting a sapling will not replace the loss of an old-growth tree in an established forest. Depending on the species, after sixty to a hundred years or more most trees are just entering adulthood and becoming more effective environmental players. Likewise, planting a new forest will not replace the loss of an old-growth one. After approximately two or three hundred years or more (according to the species) a new forest is just starting to become fully established—since it requires a second generation of naturally propagated mature trees, along with indigenous flora and fauna, to reach a more integrated state of development. This is assuming the forest is left alone and undisturbed, so that it can evolve in its own way with all its natural diversity. Without question, the Earth needs to retain what is left of its ancient trees. An ideal solution would be for governments to place all remaining old-growth forests under protection. However, as this is not going to happen, another helpful approach would be for all governments to identify remaining tracts of old-growth native forests in each ecological region to be protected and preserved in order to ensure that they are forever available to act as a nucleus for establishing future forests. Sections of such preserves could serve as nature parks to provide people with the continuing opportunity to enjoy such natural environments and experience the Earth as it once was in the fullness of its natural wild beauty.

* * *

Humans are despoiling the power of trees on Earth.
Nowhere is this more pronounced than in the thoughtless felling
of the ancient trees. It cannot be emphasized too much
that these tall trees are needed. It is not enough to reforest the
land, for young trees are not capable of conducting the higher
planetary energies; only mature trees can fulfill this task.
You cannot expect a child to perform the tasks of an adult.

The Tree Devas

COSMIC
INFLUENCES
RUDOLF STEINER, SCIENTIST & SEER

Rudolph Steiner was a spiritual teacher who lived and taught in the late 1800s and early 1900s. He developed a body of teaching that included the fields of philosophy, the arts and such practical sciences as medicine and agriculture, drawing upon both his spiritual awareness and his science background. Like other such gifted people, he could see that everything in the natural world was alive and interconnected in a vast web of life that included the cosmos. All his teachings are approached from his perspective of the subtle dimensions and provide unique insights into the life of nature and of trees.

Rudolph Steiner was born in Austria in 1861. From an early age, he was aware of the spiritual world, but when he realized that people around him did not share his awareness, he soon learned to keep his perceptions to himself. It was not until his eighteenth year, the year he graduated with distinction as a student of science and philosophy, that he finally met someone with a similar sensitivity. He chanced to meet an herb-gatherer who lived quietly in nature, away from modern civilization. The conversations he had with this man were of great importance to the young Steiner. As he later wrote, "I could speak about the spiritual world to him, as one who experienced it." This greatly boosted Steiner's confidence in his subtle perceptions and he resolved to enter more deeply into both the scientific way of thought and the supersensible dimensions that lay open to him.

In 1902, having received his doctorate and after publishing many scholarly books, Steiner began to undertake what he knew to be his life's purpose: "to found new methods of spiritual research on a scientific basis." Steiner did not want to convert people to his thinking, but hoped to present his ideas in a way that would appeal to their modern, more scientifically oriented minds, and at the same time awaken their innate intuitions. He then began to apply this approach to the various fields of philosophy, science, education and the arts. Due to the incredible demands of this work, it was not until he was nearing the end of his life that he finally addressed the issue of agriculture.

In the summer of 1924 Steiner delivered a series of eight lectures in which he sketched a broad picture of the earthly and cosmic forces involved in agriculture and provided many practical suggestions for farmers. He pictured the ideal farm as one in which soil, plants and animals exist together in a balanced relationship similar to what would be considered a viable ecosystem today.

Years later, through observations, further scientific research and practical application by Steiner's adherents, the information provided by these lectures was fleshed out and developed into today's highly successful farming methodology known as Biodynamics.

There are certain aspects of these eight lectures that relate to plant life and nature in general, and it is from them that I have chosen most of the material included here.

Cosmic Connections

Steiner begins these lectures by pointing out that in ancient times, at an earlier stage of our evolution, mankind's life was deeply integrated with the natural world and thus highly responsive to its many rhythms. Today this is no longer true, and we now experience much more freedom from the influences of the environment and the cosmos. An obvious example can be found in a woman's menstrual cycle, which imitates the lunar cycle but no longer coincides with the phases of the moon. A woman now maintains the lunar cycle within her.

This is not the case with animals, whose lives are not as emancipated from environmental influences as are ours. In the case of plants, their lives are totally immersed in the life of nature with all its rhythms. Therefore, to fully understand plants, we must realize that everything happening in their lives reflects what is taking place in nature and in the Universe at large.

An example of this can be found in the relationship between the activities of the moon and the life of plants. It is well known that lunar forces greatly affect the distribution of water on the Earth. There is a strong connection between the disbursement of the planet's water and the phases of the moon, which is quite evident in its power over ocean tides. What is less obvious is the effect that the moon's phases have on the lives of plants.

Towards a full moon, liquids rise higher within plants than they do towards a new moon. This causes plants to contain more liquid in their upper and outer portions around the time of a full moon. In former days, when humans were much closer to these things, they would use this phenomenon to their advantage by harvesting wood or cutting hay during a new moon phase, thus ensuring that the wood or hay was dryer and of a better quality. It was also considered the best time to prune plants, since having dryer outer branches meant they would bleed less sap from the cut ends.

Early farmers also chose their planting times according to the phases of the moon. A waxing moon, when both the liquid and energy of a plant are rising upward, was considered the best time to plant above-ground crops, while during the waning moon, when a plant's energy is moving toward its roots, was considered best for planting root crops.

Many years after these lectures, adherents of Steiner's philosophy conducted agricultural studies to verify and clarify his information about the effect of the moon on plant growth. At first the results proved to be inconsistent, until a German agricultural researcher, Maria Thun, uncovered the main principles involved. After ten years of patient observation on a research farm, she discovered that the moon's influence on plant growth could be altered by other factors. She found that the moon is subject to a number of different rhythms as it orbits the Earth, including variations of high and low arcs in its daily orbits, as well as crossing the path of the sun twice each month. Her research showed that all these factors modify the moon's influence on plants. Once she included these various lunar rhythms into her equations, more consistent results were achieved in selecting the best times for germination, sowing, harvesting, etc.

Aware that Steiner had also spoken of a connection between other cosmic forces and plants, Maria began exploring that possibility. She soon discovered a relationship between the moon's activities and the constellations of the zodiac. Every two or three days the moon passes into a new constellation and, as her research showed, the influence of each one, mediated by the moon, moderates a plant's growth in a different way.

Eventually Maria Thun's studies led to the creation of the Biodynamic Planting Calendar, which provides planting advice according to lunar and planetary rhythms. It must be worked out afresh each year, and is then made available to farmers and gardeners throughout the world. With the calendar's aid, farmers can fine-tune their planting. They can select the best times for planting crops according to the part of the plant they wish to enhance—be it for its fruit, as in the case of tomatoes or corn; for its flower, as in the case of broccoli; for its leaf, as with lettuce, or for its root, as in the case of beets or carrots. The calendar also provides guidance for many other gardening activities.

In his lectures, Rudolph Steiner expanded further on the relationship between cosmic forces and plants by explaining that there are two broad categories of planetary influences. The first relates to those plants that complete their life cycles in a single growing season. Most garden and agricultural plants fall into this category. These annual plants are connected with forces from the planets that have short periods of revolution around the Sun, such as the Moon, Mercury and Venus.

The second category relates to the perennials—plants that endure for many seasons. Those with long life spans are connected to forces emanating from planets that have long periods of revolution, such as Mars, Jupiter, Saturn, Uranus and Neptune. For example, Jupiter takes almost 12 earth years to circle the sun, while Saturn takes about 29.5. It is this group of planets whose forces influence the growth of trees—those plants that have the greatest life spans.

Arborists and those who work with reforestation might find it beneficial to understand the cosmic influences of this second category, as can be seen by the following comments of Dr. Steiner: "If you wish to plant coniferous forests, where the forces of Saturn play such a significant role, the results will be different if planted in an 'ascending period' or some other period of Saturn. Those who understand these things can tell precisely from the way a plant grows if it has been planted with an understanding of cosmic forces. The quality of the wood will also reflect the way the tree has been planted. These cosmic influences at work in the whole of the universe are not evident to most eyes and are no longer understood."

The Biodynamic farmer and teacher Alex Podolinsky once told his audience (I am partly paraphrasing him here): "We are fortunate to have one of the biggest oaks I have ever seen growing next to our house, with over 180 feet of leaf coverage. If one looks at such a tree, one can feel its power, particularly in the huge, solid trunk anchored in the earth. A smaller plant of the same shape would not evoke the same feeling. Within the world of plants, the great oak has a godlike presence that might be considered akin to the quality of Jupiter among the gods of the past—for not only does the oak have Jupiter's immense serenity and power, but the planet Jupiter is also the sphere of influence for such big trees as giant oaks or beeches. If a person happened to become lost with night fast approaching and saw such a tree nearby, they would immediately be drawn to settle next to it, for people find great security being next to a large tree of this kind."

Earth Intelligence

In his lectures, Dr. Steiner states: "Within any given area of the Earth, we will find specific animal life and indigenous plants existing there. Any such area can do quite well without man, but it cannot do without its animal life. There is a peculiar intelligence at work in each district of the earth that can be tested and verified. All the various animals within a given locality will instinctively eat the right measure of what the plants in that area are able to produce for them and this will result in their providing just the right amount and kind of manure that needs to be given back to the earth. Since indigenous plants are rich in those cosmic influences acting within that area of the Earth, the animals eating them will provide the very manure most suited for the soil in which the plants are growing."

According to Steiner, each district of the Earth is able to draw to itself the types and numbers of plant and animal life needed to maintain a correct balance of activities in its particular area. He expands on this by explaining that, although the mantle of the earth is generally regarded as mere "dead mineral matter containing some organic elements, it not only contains a certain vegetative nature of its own, but an astrality as well." (We might consider the term "astrality," as it is used here, to be somewhat akin to a rudimentary "feeling-awareness.")

For example, if there is enough water in a given district, the Earth there exhibits a state similar to one of "contentment." When there is too little water, it develops one similar to "discontentment." When an area contains the right type of plants for its given type of soil, the Earth there is in balance and adopts a state of serenity. Each locality also responds to certain forces coming from the cosmos that enter into the life of its plants.

The natural world has an awareness of these "states" of the Earth's various districts, and is responsive to them. For example, when there is a need for nitrogen nature will provide legumes, such plants as clovers, alders and acacias, that are able to assimilate nitrogen from the atmosphere and fix it into the soil. In this fashion, each locality of the planet helps to regulate its own environment to maintain a state of balance.

The deva kingdom would also play an important role in all of these processes, particularly the landscape devas. Although Steiner was well aware of devas and their activities, he did not try to introduce them into this particular lecture series, possibly because the information was intended primarily to assist farmers with their agricultural practices.

Dr. Steiner's work predates Jim Lovelock's Gaia Hypothesis by about 40 years. But the views of both scientists, although arrived at through quite different approaches, have a common premise. Both recognize the Earth, or Gaia, to be a living planet having a form of intelligence that is able to regulate its living systems as required to maintain a state of homeostasis.

In these eight lectures, Rudolph Steiner has provided us with an important glimpse into another dimension of nature's workings. It is common knowledge that the processes of nature are dependent upon the activities of the sun, but rarely are we shown so clearly ways in which the natural world is influenced by the activities of the moon, the planets and stars.

A Living
Planet

In the mid 1800s, scientists from many countries began to conceive of the Earth as a living planet. In his book *Animate Earth*, the popular American ecologist Aldo Leopold proposed that we might "regard the Earth's various features—soil, mountains, rivers, atmosphere, etc.—as organs or parts of organs of a coordinated whole, each part with its definite function." He then suggested that we view the slow changes that the coordinated whole undergoes over vast ages of time as a kind of metabolic process or growth. "In such case we would have all the visible attributes of a living thing." Throughout the twentieth century a number of Russian scientists introduced concepts suggesting the Earth is a living planet. But barriers existing between the Soviet Union and the rest of the world prevented their work from becoming better known. One of the most important of these scientists was Vladimir Vernadsky, considered to be one of the founders of geochemistry, biogeochemistry and radiology. He is best known for his 1926 book *The Biosphere*, in which he hypothesized that *life* is the geological force that shapes the Earth.

The Gaia Hypothesis

In 1972, British scientist James Lovelock published his famous Gaia Hypothesis. Lovelock had been hired by NASA to develop methods for detecting the presence of life on Mars during the early stages of conceptualizing and developing the Mars Rover. After formulating a way to do this, he decided to test out his approach on our own planet.

This led him to discover or identify those environmental components and processes that are linked together in feedback loops such that the Earth is able to adjust and balance its own environmental conditions, giving proof that it is a self-regulating, living organism.

After further research, assisted by biologist Dr. Lynn Margulis, Lovelock fleshed out his initial hypothesis into scientifically proven concepts and developed it into the Gaia Theory—a theory that has since gained acceptance from many scientists. Gaia, the name he chose for his hypothesis and theory, is the name of the Greek goddess that personifies the Earth—the ancestral mother of all life.

The Gaia theory posits that the Earth functions as a single, self-regulating life-form to control global temperature, atmospheric content, ocean salinity and other factors necessary to maintain stable conditions suitable for life to persist and survive—a system similar to that of any living organism that regulates its body temperature, blood salinity, etc., in order to maintain homeostasis. For example, even though the sun's energy has increased by about 30 percent over the last four billion years, the planet has responded as a whole to maintain surface temperatures at stable, habitable levels.

The existence of a planetary homeostasis assisted through the agency of living forms had been observed previously in the field of biogeochemistry, and is being investigated also in Earth System Science and other fields. Many of the Earth's processes essential for maintaining conditions that support life depend on the interaction of living forms (microorganisms, plants and animals) with mineral elements. Evidence indicates that these living environmental processes provide a responsive, global control system that regulates Earth's biosphere, even when terrestrial or external events arise to threaten it. Whenever an imbalance begins to occur in the biosphere, one of the planet's living systems is triggered to increase or decrease its activities in response and thus to bring about balance. Needless to say, foremost among the planet's living systems of regulation are its trees and forests, which need to be preserved in sufficient numbers if they are to adequately fulfill this role.

It is interesting to note that the more science advances in its understanding of the natural world, the more its views begin to reflect the world-view of aboriginal peoples. It is their belief that a Supreme

Power or Great Spirit created Mother Earth as a living planet, and that all aspects of it are forms of life that share in its Life-force.

The concept that the Earth is a living planet is gaining wider acceptance today. But what is the nature of such a form of life? As David Spangler writes in his book *Partnering with Earth*: "Our own body has such regulatory systems as well, which serve to keep us within a particular temperature range and which adjust various other chemical and hormonal balances within our bodies. But we experience ourselves as much more than just the sum total of their operation. We experience will, purpose, the capacity to imagine and to think, the felt sense of an identity. We experience a self that is more than the simple totality of bodily processes.

"Gaia is a living soul, a planetary spirit, holding in itself resources of will and purpose that foster the evolution of life and consciousness within and upon its planetary body. The nature of this spirit and its level of consciousness may be beyond our capacity to fully understand, but on the other hand, it is a sentient field within which we participate."

Within Gaia's earth-body, the devas are the intermediaries that perform all its regulatory activities; for their work lies not only with the various lives of nature, but also with the life forces of the Earth as a whole. It is a work that involves great planetary and cosmic energies. There is no better example of these global activities than the work they become involved with each year towards the end of December.

During the time that marks the close of one year and the birth of another, there is a great surge in the activities within the Deva realm. Each year, around the time of Advent, there is a global renewal process that begins with a tremendous outflow of energies from the center of the Earth to its circumference. These cleansing, purifying and creative forces are part of a planetary process that helps prepare the earth for a huge inflow of new life energies from the Cosmos that enter towards the end of December. As this cosmic outpouring enters into the life of the Earth and nature, dynamic energies of life are released that will eventually cause the planet to burst into blossom in the spring. Hierarchies of devas facilitate these global processes by controlling, balancing and distributing the energies involved.

In ancient times, all religions were aligned with the activities of the natural world and recognized this cosmic event—now known in the west as Christmas—to be an important time of the year and celebrated it with special ceremonies. These ceremonies, which are still part of organized religions today (although not recognized as such), were crafted to coincide with the various stages of this planetary renewal of life and were performed to provide human assistance, as well as to celebrate them.

Gaia, Christmas and Santa

In the western world, Christmas is associated with northern cultures and there is a reason for this. For many great ages, the north has been the center receiving this annual influx of new life. The south, on the other hand, has been the recipient of balancing energies that are important to provide a deepening of this life into form. The northern hemisphere holds certain "inner channels" that receive the inflow of these creative energies that help shape the evolution of both nature and man. It is a process that involves hosts of devas to receive and distribute these energies—a flood of new life that enters at the north and then flows southward to impregnate the entire planet towards the end of each year.

The myth of Santa Claus, associated with this time, is a kind of folk legend that has emerged out of ancient customs and myths that predate Christianity. The modern version seems to be a mixture of the Norse and German pagan festival of Yule, the 270 A.D. figure of Saint Nicholas the Generous, Father Christmas of Britain, and in the Netherlands, Sinterklaas, which became anglicized into Santa Claus after crossing the Atlantic. Eventually the date was moved to December 25th to coincide with Christ Mass. Its current North American form emerged from the classic 1882 children's poem "The Night Before Christmas" by American writer Clement Moore, in which he created a delightful mix of all these elements.

But the reason these seasonal folk celebrations have persisted, while continually adapting new forms, is because they are rooted in a deeper reality. One can find evidence of that reality in the various components that are part of these customs and celebrations today.

Nicholas of Myra, the bringer of gifts, is possibly the most common human personification of Christmas. It was said that he went about at night dressed in his red bishop's cloak depositing coins in the shoes of poor children, who would leave them out for that purpose. Children are usually a part of this festival as they represent mankind's new life and hope for the future. Both Saint Nicholas and Father Christmas are often depicted in a red or green cloak, carrying a sack of gifts and a small evergreen tree. Why a tree? Or, for that matter, why do we have Christmas trees? From earliest times, the tree has been a universal symbol of life and renewal. The tree of life at this time is the Christmas tree, a northern conifer filled with light and surrounded with gifts for all and holding a promise of good things to come.

The magical ride of Santa Claus is a wonderful metaphor for this yearly renewal of planetary life. The jolly old elf, a generous and joy-filled nature being that dwells at the north pole with an army of elven helpers, sweeps out of the north at Christmastime carrying with him a bounty of gifts that he then distributes to the entire world. It is a mythic folk tale that reflects and celebrates the annual outflow of cosmic life energies from the northern hemisphere into the rest of the planet—a gift of fresh new life for the Earth.

* * *

Gaia is a living soul,
a planetary spirit, holding in itself
resources of will and purpose
that foster the evolution of life
and consciousness within and upon
its planetary body.

David Spangler

THE PROMISE
OF FINDHORN

Sooner or later mankind will have to acknowledge its part in crippling the planet's biosphere and the governments of the world will have to join forces and work together to develop strategies for regenerating sufficient natural areas to restore our planet's health. At such time it would be highly beneficial if the forces of nature were included as partners in these environmental efforts.

There are prophecies suggesting that, at some future time, mankind and the deva kingdom will join forces and begin to work together cooperatively in full consciousness. The possibilities that this holds for restoring the natural environment are enormous. For anyone who may doubt the value of such collaboration, a preview of its potential influence on plant growth was demonstrated in the early days of Findhorn, when direct conscious cooperation with the deva realm produced a remarkable garden on a sand dune.

As mentioned in a previous chapter, the three founders of the Findhorn community began their garden in a trailer park in the spring of 1963. Having never gardened before, Peter Caddy began to dig an initial small plot to help provide for the group's needs. The soil he encountered there was comprised of extremely fine sand overlying gravel and sand. It was so fine that it was quite difficult to water, since moisture would simply "bead" on the surface. Locals often had poor gardening results.

The deva realm cooperated in the project by offering advice whenever

Dorothy Maclean approached them with gardening questions, and by directing vital energies into the garden. Peter was an energetic and forceful individual with natural organizing skills. He had complete faith in both Eileen and Dorothy's messages and any gardening advice received from the devas by Dorothy was accepted and put into practice immediately.

They were advised to avoid all chemical fertilizers or pesticides in the garden and to create compost using only natural materials. Having almost no cash, the group had to rely on whatever materials they could find in order to build the compost. But they always managed to obtain everything they needed in extraordinary ways—such as discovering a load of spilled manure one morning on the roadside, almost next to their property.

In the very first year the group produced a garden of outstanding vigor and productivity that astounded their neighbors, particularly as their large cabbages and Brussels sprouts were the only ones in the area to survive an infestation of cabbage-root grubs. Likewise, they had a healthy and abundant black currant harvest, while crops largely failed in the rest of the county.

The following season they enlarged the garden and planted twenty fruit trees. By May of the following year the fruit trees were bursting into bud. In June of that year, a county horticulture adviser came to take a sample of their soil for analysis. While doing so, he advised Peter that the soil would require at least two ounces of potash per square yard. Peter told him that he didn't believe in artificial fertilizers and relied on compost. The adviser assured him that compost would prove to be quite inadequate. But six weeks later, when he returned with the results of the analysis, the adviser appeared quite mystified. The analysis showed that the soil was without deficiencies and contained all necessary elements, including rare trace elements. He then tried to persuade Caddy to join him for an interview on BBC Radio to discuss their garden.

In 1967 Eileen Caddy received a suggestion in her meditation to enlarge the garden and to include many kinds of flowers in order to make it a place of beauty. The beds of flowers they then planted were treated in the same way as the vegetables and developed an outstanding color and vibrancy. The whole enlarged garden was now lush and beautiful.

By 1968, rumors of it had reached gardening experts. Those who came to check it out for themselves praised the exceptional vitality and bounty they found there and spread the word to other gardeners. After her first visit to the garden in that year, Elizabeth Murray, an organic gardener and member of the highly respected Soil Association, remarked, "The radiant health of the fruits, vegetables, flowers and trees were far beyond the ordinary, and the superior size, quality and flavor of their superb produce could not be explained by compost thinly spread over sand."

Lady Mary, sister of the founder of the Soil Association, then paid a brief visit during a grey, damp September day and was astonished by the extraordinary brilliance of the flowers in bloom there. "And they all seemed to be in bloom!" she later wrote. "The flower beds were a compact mass of colour and form in great variety. The effect was riotous and weed-free but harmonious. I stooped to handle and examine the soil, a thickish layer of half-ripe compost mulching on the rather grimy, too-fine sand below. To my eye and touch it was indeed pure sand of the most unpromising quality."

Lady Mary's impressions of the garden spread quickly within the Soil Association and inspired many more members to visit. The following winter, Professor R. Lindsay Robb, a United Nations agricultural expert and lecturer of agriculture at several universities, as well as a consultant to the Soil Association, visited Findhorn and afterward went on public record to write, "The vigor, health and bloom of the plants in the garden at midwinter on land that is almost a barren powdery sand cannot be explained by the moderate dressings of compost, nor indeed by the application of any known cultural methods of organic husbandry. There are other factors present and they are vital ones."

Finally, Lady Eve Balfour, the Soil Association's founder, decided she must see the garden for herself. Her response was no different from the others. As she later wrote, "I have seen gardens as good on big estates going for hundreds of years, attended by teams of gardeners, but never one better!"

Some visitors were sceptics who came to check out the veracity of the "overblown" stories of the garden. And then there were the disgruntled, reluctant men that were dragged there by their enthusiastic mates. Peter

recognised one such unhappy male trailing his wife through the flower garden one afternoon and went out to see if they had any questions. The man was a Church of England minister who soon told Peter that he thought the whole thing was utter nonsense. As he continued to talk, it became evident that he was one of England's top rose experts.

In her meditations, Eileen had been advised that every person who came to their garden had something to offer. So then and there, Peter invited the minister to design a rose garden to border the road. Surprisingly, he agreed to this and later that year sent Peter a detailed plan that specified each variety of rose and where it was to be located. Peter had to send south for many of them and that winter he planted them all according to the plan. When the minister paid a visit the following summer he was most surprised to find a bank of vibrant roses in full bloom that included every variety he had specified. He was quite mystified by this for, as he then confessed to Peter, "I included roses that I knew couldn't possibly grow in this climate and soil."

Around the same time, a newspaper article revealed that the Findhorn group was in touch with and cooperating with intelligences of nature. News of the "miracle garden" and of the community's conscious cooperation with nature quickly spread worldwide via the media. Before long, people from many countries began traveling to northern Scotland to visit it.

The publicity also attracted like-minded people who wanted to join them. This was the beginning of their development into a community. By 1970 there were about 20 permanent members in the community and by the end of 1972 there were more than 120.

As it grew, with many people working in the gardens, Dorothy received suggestions from her inner sources of ways the energies of people and devas might blend more effectively when working with nature. The gardeners were advised to think of their work in terms of "radiation" and it was emphasized that the most important thing they could do while working in the garden was to radiate love and appreciation to the plants, as this would assist them far more effectively than fertilizer. Another deva message expanded on this theme, adding:

Every gardener contributes to his garden in this way unconsciously, but those who are consciously aligned can contribute much more. Certain people can stimulate plant growth, while some have a depressing effect and draw forces from the plants. Happiness has an especially good effect on plants, and children's playing does as well. Our radiations are interwoven much more than you realize.

This may explain why some individuals are considered to have "green thumbs." Quite likely they are people who greatly enjoy being in nature and naturally radiate love and appreciation while working with plants. I'm sure we all know someone like this, and have seen how well the plants in their gardens and homes respond to their care.

Cooperation with the Forces of Nature

In the years following her days at Findhorn, Dorothy Maclean traveled throughout the world, giving lectures and workshops. During these events she often tried to encourage those attending to try attuning to the subtle levels of the nature world. She was certain that more people could do what she did if only they would believe that they could and then take the time to try.

"Each one of us has the capacity to tune in to these angelic realms," she writes, and then quotes a suggestion given to her by one of her deva sources:

Just tune in to nature until you feel the love flow. That is your arrow into the deva world. It does not matter if there is a message or not, it is the state which counts. Always it is your state that the nature world responds to, not what you say, not what you do, but what you are.

When faced with difficult environmental situations, the local landscape deva can be quite helpful. "Landscape deva" is the name Dorothy used when referring to these overarching beings. But they might also be thought of as "ecosystem devas," since the activities of nature within each ecosystem are somewhat unique and each is presided over by its own deva. These intelligences understand the state of an area and all its relationships—both within and with surrounding environments. They are capable of directing to it the forces required to assist and balance these relationships and to enhance plant vitality, but always in accordance with the blueprints of Creation.

One way to enter into relationship with one of these beings is to take a quiet time to think of this deva and to invite its assistance in the planning and undertaking of a project. This can help pave the way for a fuller collaboration and for achieving better results. Then, if we go about the various tasks with an open mind and a willingness to learn from nature itself, it may result in receiving insights for new and better ways to perform the work.

No matter what approach is taken in an environmental project, the way one relates to the plants involved will greatly influence results. Of primary importance is to treat them with love and respect. This was explained many times to Dorothy in her deva exchanges, such as in this one:

Do you know that every thought of mankind about a plant makes contact with the nature world? It is not a great contact and it is not lasting, but nevertheless, humans in their thought world cross into our world. If you realized just how much your thoughts impinge on others and on other worlds, you might be more careful, for your thoughts are indeed far-reaching. All thoughts have influences for they are life-moving, and how often do they move in a positive direction? Blessed are the pure in thought—and powerful, too.

Does this seem a little far-fetched? Is there any solid evidence to confirm it? As mentioned earlier, Cleve Backster was possibly the first scientist to verify how sensitive plants are to human thoughts by his experiments with a polygraph instrument. The scientist Marcel Vogel, being skeptical of these findings, conducted similar experiments of his own. When they corroborated Backster's results, he became intrigued and went on to make further discoveries. In one experiment, Marcel picked three leaves from an elm tree and placed them on a plate of glass. Each day, for one minute, he focused love on the two outer leaves while carefully ignoring the center leaf. After a week the outer leaves were still green and healthy looking, while the inner leaf had shriveled and turned brown. Using similar methods, Vogel's colleagues were able to keep leaves green and alive for over two months.

If we wish to promote the vitality and growth of plants, it is evident that love is the magic elixir that they respond to most—a lesson Findhorn had to learn more than once. On several occasions, when plants in the garden were not doing well, the devas pointed to their need for love and attention. Here are a couple of such examples: When Peter Caddy planted the first Horse Chestnut tree in their garden, the three founders welcomed it, blessed it and enjoyed watching it thrive and develop. Later, it became necessary to move the young tree. The move was undertaken with care and sensitivity but, as Dorothy writes, "It did not grow as well as in its previous position." When she approached the Deva of the Horse

Chestnut about the little tree, she received this response:

As you know, we joined in the joy of the move and were grateful for all the solicitude shown. One of the reasons that this tree thrived so much in its previous position was that you were all continuously passing, admiring and blessing it. In its present position it is out of the way and if it is to thrive equally here, you will have to go out of your way to pass it and give it love. We, of course, will play our part in caring for it, and hope you will do the same.

This next example relates to a situation that was significant to the future of the entire garden. In their early days at Findhorn, Peter, Eileen and Dorothy were all deeply involved with the creation and development of the garden. But as Findhorn began to grow and expand, they became ever more involved with the demands of the growing community. As a result, their focus on the garden necessarily began to diminish and they had to rely more and more on the help of community members and the many transient visitor volunteers to take care of the gardens. Even though steps were taken to pass on their experiences to the new teams of gardeners, the vibrancy of the gardens began to show a change. Eventually, Dorothy became aware of the situation and when she questioned the Findhorn landscape deva about it, received this response:

The devas and nature spirits are more than willing to cooperate with you in the garden as we have already proven for all to see, that with this cooperation the impossible can be achieved—but it is a matter of cooperation. If you do not play your part, then the garden will revert to an ordinary one as has already begun. We know you are busy. We know your energies are called upon in other directions, and we have taken this into account, but we also have given certain fundamental guidance that has yet to be accepted and acted upon; therefore, we must withhold our miracles.

With the new gardeners, we hope that much can be rectified, but we do miss the energies you had given to us before. Besides love and caring, more compost heaps would help.

We hope that joy will return to the garden. It is here, to be brought down with your help.

In this and a few other communications, the deva realm made it quite clear that the garden of Findhorn did not achieve its splendor solely due to their input. As they explained, it never could have achieved its magical results without the fullness of love, care and attention provided by its human creators and caregivers.

There is an important and fundamental lesson here. Love is a universal energy that nurtures, empowers and uplifts every living thing. Just as our children and animals happily thrive when given plenty of loving support and care, so do plants. The problem is most people are unaware that plants are sentient lives, responsive to human thoughts and feelings, and so fail to treat them accordingly.

It is a prevalent human failing to undervalue the natural abilities that we all possess. Human love seems much too common and mundane, while the idea of benevolent angels with magical powers seems far more appealing. The remarkable bounty of Findhorn's early garden was, in fact, a co-creative venture—the result of cooperative efforts and loving input by both humans and devas.

As events continued to unfold, Findhorn developed into a large, international new age educational center. The three founders were fully involved in tasks related to the challenges of its evolving community affairs and did not choose to return to their former gardening activities. Findhorn had now changed its focus. It had entered a new phase and had become "a garden of people," as Peter Caddy liked to express it. The experiences, insights and revelations gained in those eight intensive years of gardening became foundational elements in the life principles and patterns of the new community and in its educational programs.

It was in this second stage of its development that Findhorn gained its international recognition. Articles began to appear in many forms of media. Peter Tompkins visited and then included it in his popular book *The Secret Life of Plants*. An article derived from this book appeared in *Harper's Magazine*. BBC filmed it four different times—the final one was a one-hour prime-time television special. Paul Hawken's 1975 book *The Magic of Findhorn* created considerable interest, especially in North America. Findhorn had gained world-wide recognition. The early garden with its extraordinary produce, such as its "famous" forty-pound cabbage, was now part of its history. But it had fulfilled its purpose for, as the devas explained, a primary reason for the original garden's remarkable bounty, and for their extra efforts there, was to provide a demonstration of future possibilities and to show what is possible and will become more common in the future when an awakened humanity begins to work in conscious collaboration with the intelligences of nature.

I met Peter and Eileen Caddy several different times in the early 1980s. On one of those occasions, during a conversation with Eileen about their original garden, she paused and, with a faraway look in her eyes, mused, "If only someone had thought to take a picture of that cabbage."

* * *

BIG TREES
IN THE
BIG PICTURE

Like the planet, forests are sentient, self-regulating entities and it is time we changed our thinking as to their nature. The study of ecology is a relatively modern but rapidly advancing science, primarily concerned with understanding the interactivity and interdependence of organisms with each other and with their environment. Today, it is becoming more widely accepted by ecologists and other scientists that forests are living systems whose components function with an interconnected awareness that allows the whole to maintain a healthy and balanced state. This is no different than that of any organism, including our physical bodies. It is well understood that when our bodies are no longer able to maintain a state of balance we become dysfunctional and can develop illnesses. This is true of all living systems including ecosystems such as forests.

In order to maintain homeostasis, forests display an ability to work in group fashion to detect imbalances and then select and pursue strategies for correcting them. There need to be more studies to fully understand the different roles of the great numbers of interdependent lives that make up established forests. But some individuals have studied forests as living systems and have already discovered the basics. As Dr. Suzanne Simard explains so well: "Like humans and most living things, trees build families, form relationships and thrive best when surrounded by a diverse community of species and genotypes." And she has found that the mature "mother" or hub trees of a forest, which may be linked to hundreds of other trees, are key to its well-being. "You can take out

one or two hub trees, but there is a tipping point," says Simard. "You take out one too many and the whole system collapses."

Let's look at certain fundamentals: the plant kingdom stands at the foundations of life. It is the root source of food for most living things in the planet's chain of life. Plants have the alchemical ability to transform earth, air, fire and water into living tissue. They are able to harness the light of the fiery sun and use it to metabolize minerals from the soil, carbon dioxide and other gases from the air and water from the ground to help create and maintain a stable atmosphere and an environment suitable for life on earth.

Trees are the highest developed members of the plant kingdom, and especially in their forest communities, are primary players in most planetary life processes. They lift and maintain water tables, help to build and protect topsoil, help balance oxygen-carbon dioxide ratios, purify air and water, nurture water systems, feed and house countless life-forms, help to regulate Earth's temperatures and weather patterns. And there are other vital services provided by trees that mankind does not yet understand.

Peace, Stability and Upliftment

In all these life processes, the big tree elders play key roles, particularly in those requiring size, strength and experience. Moreover, just by their presence, the large older trees provide a gift to the world; for mature trees embody and radiate into their environment the qualities of serene peace, stability and groundedness—qualities badly needed by every person and everything that lives in and around today's hectic urban areas. Just enter a mature forest and you will experience this for yourself. No therapy system will calm and balance a person more effectively than will a quiet walk in an established forest. These beneficial qualities that mature trees possess and radiate into their environment were pointed out many times to Dorothy in her exchanges with trees devas. Here are several examples:

We bless all who come into our aura and rest, but our life is not felt consciously by those of you who are so self-absorbed that you are closed to our qualities. Nevertheless, all are influenced on certain levels; you cannot come into our forests without part of you synchronizing with that which is common to us both.

It would be most beneficial if large woodlands were retained near every city, for trees have a special gift to offer man in this age of speed and change. They embody the qualities of peace, strength, stability and continuity. They bless all who come and rest within their aura. Their serene strength provides an aura of groundedness and upliftment to all life throughout the world. Where there is a dearth of large trees, the peace and stability of mankind is also affected. For all lives are deeply connected.

Our peace reaches from earth to Heaven, from cosmic heights to the depth of matter. Often we have reminded you that you too can find this peace through us and through what you have of us within you. Linger in the forests. Linger near us. Healing comes when you do.

We are so immersed in our rapidly developing world of technology that there is little awareness of the ways in which the large, older trees affect us, simply by their serene presence. But they do, whether we are aware of it or not. There is a fine example of the healing power of an ancient tree's presence in a recent book by Dr. Stuart Shanker, entitled *Self-Reg* and published by Penguin Press. In this book, which deals with helping disturbed children break free of the stress cycle, Dr. Shanker relates what he describes as the most powerful lesson he has learned about how to break a stress cycle.

While visiting and studying the work of a children's agency in western Australia, he met "Stan," an Aboriginal healer who worked with troubled teens. They were often kids that tried to harm themselves, and most were battling such addictions as drinking alcohol or sniffing gas. After a few exchanges related to their work and experiences, Stan offered to show Dr. Stuart his clinic. They then set off on a walk that wound through a natural area teeming with birds and wildlife.

In about twenty minutes they arrived at a small clearing dominated by a huge baobab—a tree more than 1500 years old that is native to western Australia. Like most of these ancient trees, it was only about twenty feet tall but with an enormous girth. Although the air was filled with the noises of kookaburras, herons and other birds, Dr. Shanker describes it as "one of the most peaceful settings I have ever encountered."

Stan and he sat down side by side under the tree and remained there quiet and immersed in the tranquility for some time. Although it was the end of a busy day, Dr. Stuart suddenly felt refreshed, alert and eager to explore ideas that were emerging in his mind. When he mentioned these changes he was experiencing to Stan, the latter nodded in agreement and explained that this was how he worked with agitated teens and especially kids that were "shut down." He would just sit with them under the tree until they felt like talking. In some cases, it might take a full day, but eventually they would all open up and quietly begin to talk about their troubles.

From his experience of sitting in that natural setting, Dr. Stuart realized the reason it was such an effective "clinic" for working with troubled teens was because of the atmosphere of equanimity and calm that the ancient baobab tree provided—it instilled in the kids "a feeling

of emotional safety and security" and this allowed them to relax and open up.

Like the Planet's Skin

Many people have some familiarity with the views of today's scientists regarding the state of the Earth and its environment. But, since we are neither aware of nor understand the vast subtle dimensions that lie outside our physical senses that yet are a major part of our world, very few have any knowledge of the views of their inhabitants. This includes the Deva Kingdom that work directly with the formative forces of Creation and possesses an intimate understanding of the vital interdependence of every form of life—planetary, cosmic and spiritual. If we were able to see the world from their perspective, the dangerous imbalances being created today by the loss of the planet's big trees would be starkly evident, as was suggested to Dorothy Maclean by the deva of the Monterey Cypress.

Perhaps if you were in tune with all of Creation, as we are, and doing your part, the forces of the earth would be balanced, but at present the planet needs more than ever just what is being destroyed—the very forces that go through the lordly trees. The world needs us on a large scale.

Native forests are essential components of our living planet. They are its most important terrestrial ecosystems and home to 80 percent of its biodiversity, including plants, animals and microorganisms. It is difficult to imagine how the continuing disappearance of old-growth forests and big trees must be affecting the activities of the nature spirits and devas that work with them. We know that without trees in sufficient numbers, they are very hampered in their work. Possibly their situation might be similar to that of a ground control crew trying to do its part in maintaining the functioning of a space station that has missing parts and damaged instruments. In this questionable analogy, the Earth is the space station and we are its passengers, along with all the plants and animals of the planet. We are also the ones blindly damaging or removing parts of the station and creating ever-increasing difficulties for it to maintain its stability and life-support functions.

Trees have been around for about 370 million years and are found throughout the Earth—some in places where few living organisms can survive. By the 1950s, after vast acres of forests had been cleared by human activities, it was estimated the planet still hosted approximately 3 trillion adult trees that covered approximately 30 percent of its land. By the early 2000s this number had dropped to around 5 percent. Planet Earth is a living organism that has successfully evolved over countless millennia, and if it once held trees in such huge numbers, we can be assured that there must be good reasons for this.

There are, as we know, many reasons, but there is an important one that mankind does not seem to have the least awareness of. Many of the messages that Dorothy received from tree devas stressed the necessity for mankind to understand that trees function much like a "skin" to the planet. Here is one such message received from the Leylands Cypress deva:

Trees function like the skin of the Earth, and a skin not only covers and protects, but also passes through it the forces of life. Nothing could be more vital to the life of the planet than trees.

What might this mean? Certainly, trees cover vast areas of the planet and protect it with their root networks and canopy of foliage, but what are the potent forces that pass through them into the Earth? To better understand this, we need to recognize that the Earth also lives within a type of ecosystem—a planetary and cosmic ecosystem. Just as it is impossible for any creature to survive long without the environment and milieu that supports it, so it is for planet Earth. It is part of a cosmic community in which it has relationships and energetic exchanges with our sun and neighboring planets, as well as with certain stellar bodies. The true science of astrology (as opposed to the popular form) deals with some of these cosmic relationships and exchanges.

And what does this have to do with trees? Communications from the deva realm stress that the Earth requires the antennae-like presence of big, deep-rooted trees in great numbers for it to properly receive, transform and ground the energies involved in these extra-planetary

exchanges.

They also explain that many of these subtle cosmic forces are best handled by the larger and older trees since they, with their maturity, strength and experience, have the developed capacity that enables them not only to receive and handle these higher energies, but also to appropriately modify them for the planet's use before conducting them through their root systems into the earth. This has been explained by many of the tree devas who have been trying to bring this issue to mankind's attention—in this case, through their communications with Dorothy.

Although quoted in an earlier chapter, the following message received in 1968 from the Findhorn landscape deva is included here again, since it expresses this issue so clearly.

Large trees are conductors of energy; they stand ever ready, channeling the universal forces that surround and are part of the world. These trees are carriers of especially potent vibrations, sentinels of cosmic energy, transforming this power and conducting it into the Earth. Young trees are not capable of conducting the higher planetary energies; only mature trees can fulfill this task.

As yet, we do not know the exact nature or purpose of these extra-planetary forces, but they are deserving of serious scientific investigation. Over fifty years ago, the deva kingdom began trying to alert mankind, through Dorothy, that the reception and distribution of these cosmic forces are essential for the proper functioning of the planet, and that the large, older trees needed to receive and channel them are already in short supply. A young sapling will not be able to appropriately handle these cosmic energies until after sixty years or more of growth.

Our big trees are precious and essential, not only for the well-being of the forests, but also for the well-being of Gaia and all the lives it supports. With each passing year, the need to preserve what remains of them becomes increasingly more urgent. It is in our own best interest to see that all remaining old-growth trees and ancient wilderness areas are preserved and that more of our forests be allowed to regenerate to the fullness and diversity of their former wild state.

***

Vast areas need us, and by us, I mean large trees in general. We simply cannot emphasize this enough. We are the skin of this world; take us away and the complete planet, no longer able to function, dries up and dies. Leave us be and the whole planet hums with contentment, and life goes on in its natural sequence.

Deva of the Lawson's Cypress

A Time
Of Change

The day is not too far off when an awareness of the true value of our trees and forests will become more widespread and awaken public concern. In fact, this awakening is already beginning to happen, as is evidenced by the greater number of environmental activities under way throughout the world today. A recognized need for change is "in the air" and is now working its way into all levels of society, with the result that both governments and industries in many countries are already taking notice and some are beginning to respond. As is often said today, "people power" is on the rise, and people are becoming less and less willing to accept seeing their world controlled by authoritarian structures and material interests.

Here is a good example of the effectiveness of people power. For many years environmental groups, frustrated by the lack of government action to address the plight of the boreal woodland caribou, had been harassing and pressing the forestry industry to green their processes and improve their reputations by submitting to the Forest Stewardship Council (FSC) certification program. The FSC is an international inspection system that guarantees forest products bearing their label come from forests that are responsibly managed.

About a decade before the signing of the Boreal Agreement and after years of public campaigns that had little impact, environmental groups became more sophisticated and shifted the focus of their campaigns from the forestry companies to the largest buyers of their products—the major forestry products retailers. These included such companies as IKEA (one of the world's largest users of wood), Kimberly-Clarke (world's largest tissue manufacturer) and Home Depot (North America's largest lumber retailer.) The environmental groups launched public campaigns accusing these market-sensitive retailers of using or selling wood products from forestry companies that were destroying northern forests, and with them, the habitat of the endangered woodland caribou.

Up until this point, public concerns about the plight of the endangered caribou had no way of influencing events, since forestry companies were quite immune to public opinion. But this was not the case with the retailers. People power now entered the picture as retailers began receiving bad press and questions from concerned customers. In a relatively short period of time, the campaign proved to be so effective that it was the primary factor that caused all twenty-one forestry companies to commit to FSC certification as part of the Boreal Agreement.

The power of people's opinions, interests and lifestyles to influence change can be found everywhere today. I spotted an article in the newspaper recently entitled, "Companies turn to green policies as climate change threatens profits." It reported a study showing that "companies behind best-known consumer products" are beginning to factor climate change into their business equation to bolster their green credentials. The article explains that they are doing this because they are beginning to feel the heat of climate activism, and because they are now facing increasing scrutiny from investors who want to know what business risks from climate change a company faces before deciding whether to buy its stock. A week later, another article appeared stating that most companies are projected to face record numbers of climate-change-related proposals from shareholders in annual meetings this season.

These evidences of a growing change in humanity's outlook are a welcome sign. It is clear that we will have to make many major changes in our ways if forests are ever to regain an adequate foothold on the planet. However, this may happen sooner than we think. The most obvious catalyst is climate change itself, which is now beginning to exert its presence quite forcibly into our lives everywhere. And there is also another less obvious factor at work. Part of the growing change in public mood is due to the influence of larger, unseen forces, for the times they are a-changin'.

A Time of Reawakening

At an earlier stage of human evolution, as Rudolph Steiner and others have explained, mankind enjoyed an entirely different relationship with the natural world. In those ancient times, prior to the fuller development of human mental faculties, we were less mentally focused but more open or aware in our subtle senses. This made our intimate links with nature and the cosmos quite evident to us—not because we were more astute, but because we were aware of these things and accepted them as a natural part of our daily lives.

Over the ages, as we have evolved greater mental aptitude, we have become increasingly immersed in and ruled by our concepts— even when those concepts differ from the reality lying before us. At the same time, we began "losing our senses" as our awareness of the subtle dimensions faded into the background of our consciousness. Our growing conceptual perceptions, which tend to shape one's daily reality, also began to marginalize and eventually to disclude our connectedness to nature and to the cosmos, due to a lack of "hard" evidence. But these subtle senses did not disappear, although the majority of people today no longer are aware of them. They are still part of us and available to us today, if we wish to take the time and effort to reawaken them.

At present, our world is in the difficult transition period between two different "ages"—two quite different periods of civilization. This is causing much of the turmoil and political division we are witnessing today. Some people are responding to the newer qualities and values that are being ushered in by the new Aquarian Age, while others are resisting and holding on to the values and ways of the receding Piscean Age.

As we enter more deeply into the Aquarian era, there will be increasing numbers of people "coming to their senses." But it will not be the same as in earlier times. On this leg of mankind's evolutionary journey, these subtle senses will be partnered with more highly developed mental faculties. And, as this Age continues to unfold and this trend continues to grow, it will eventually awaken humankind to an awareness of the reality of the subtle dimensions, the vital other half of our world—for one cannot exist without the other. This will slowly transform human civilizations into societies more integrated with both nature and the subtle realms.

We have come a long way in our understanding of the natural world. Our environmental scientists have uncovered a mountain of information and insights about the ecosystems of our planet, and we are at last beginning to tap into some of the aboriginal wisdom of the land. Only greed and ignorance stand in the way of our taking effective action today to begin restoring the planet's natural environment.

Although the forces of materialism seem to be dominating human affairs at present, "this too shall pass," as the saying goes. Change is inevitable, for as planet Earth swings ever deeper into the sphere of influence of the constellation Aquarius, Gaia and all lives in it and upon it will become increasingly immersed in and influenced by Aquarian qualities—those of synthesis and unity. In mankind, these qualities will be expressed as humanitarianism, brotherhood of man, and a universalism that respects and honors all living things. Since such qualities don't fit well with activities of separatism, nationalism, selfishness and exploitation, further changes are as inevitable as the tide and are just a matter of time. For, as the proverb states: "Time and tide wait for no man."

In time, mankind will awaken to the essential role of the natural world and begin to appreciate and honor it for its priceless gifts of life.

In time, mankind will acknowledge its part in creating the environmental problems facing us and will turn its creative genius toward the task of healing and restoring Earth's air, waters, forests and other natural areas, drawing upon a deeper understanding of nature and ecology.

Over time, there will be increasing numbers of people on Earth with awakened subtle senses that will enter into communication with the inhabitants of the subtle realms. This will lead to wide-scale cooperation between Earth's two most evolved intelligences, deva and mankind, and open the door for achieving miraculous results in restoring and revitalising Gaia's natural environments—even greater than those attained in the early garden of Findhorn. But let's give the last word on this to the devas, with their timeless perspective:

We have stressed, and your religions have stressed, that you love one another, but these words have been just words to you. The plant world responds immediately to what is directed at it, for it has no barriers of mind or self to resist or twist what comes its way, and love directed to it has a tremendous power—truly tremendous and yet sensitive.

It is said that God is love. This is so, and as Creation becomes more conscious, it expresses greater love. The essence of life, no matter what its form of consciousness, is love and therefore, when it is surrounded in love, it becomes more truly itself and is more perfectly itself. This is true of all kingdoms, and man's greatest contribution to the planet and to all life on it is to consciously give forth love, which brings health, vigor, beauty and perfection to all life.

Love is a firm reality that forms a bridge over which all can walk. Syrupy sentiment is not love and does not exist with us. We stand here in love, a whole dynamic world reaching for an intelligent relationship with a humanity that will wield all its God-given forces for the good of the whole.

In the past, plants have been forced and even tortured to bring about certain results. Far greater results will be joyfully achieved with love. As you believe in and wield the power of love, you will see this happen, because there is no greater power.

The gardens of the future will far surpass anything known at present, not because science and intelligence aid or promote them, but because love does—for sensitivity and sharing of love nurtures a plant to its fullness, to its highest perfection or its God-qualities. In the coming age, humans will more fully express their God-qualities. As love surrounds them, plants will more quickly express their God-qualities with more openness to change and in greater harmony with the rest of life. Plant miracles will happen, because love is a miracle-worker.

The Landscape Deva of Findhorn

Acknowledgments

Special thanks to my editor, Margaret Carney, whose encouragement, reflections and advice were invaluable to me in the shaping of this book. Many thanks also to my talented designer, Rebecca Barclay, who has made the book so pleasing to the eye. And thanks to Ann Miller, who gave freely of her time to review my writing and provide helpful feedback. I must also thank Freya Secrest, who always responded promptly to my requests for information and opinions, and to Jeremy Berg, who has been a guiding light in all my publishing journeys. And, of course, I thank my wife, Liz, for putting up with my frequent mental absences as I slipped into and out of writing mode either in my mind or at the computer.

Bibliography

Bailey, Alice A. *A Treatise on Cosmic Fire*. Lucis Publishing Company, 1973.

Baker, Richard St. Barbe. *My Life My Trees*. Findhorn Press, 1981.

Baker, Richard St. Barbe. *Man of the Trees*. Ecology Action, 1989.

Beresford-Kroeger, Diana. *The Global Forest, 40 Ways Trees Can Save Us*. Penguin Books, 2011.

Beresford-Kroeger, Diana. *Arboretum Borealis, A Lifeline of the Planet*. The University of Michigan Press, 2013.

Beresford-Kroeger, Diana. *Arboretum Americana: A Philosophy of the Forest*. The University of Michigan Press, 2015.

Biography.com. Wangari Maathai. www.biography.com/people/wangari-maathai-13704918

Coghlan, Andy. "More Crops for Africa as Trees Reclaim the Desert." *New Scientist*, 2006.

Granger, Alan. "The Disappearing Rain Forest." *The Ecologist*.

Hawken, Paul. *The Magic of Findhorn*. Harper & Row, 1975.

Liu, John D. "Loess Plateau Watershed Rehabilitation Project." Environmental Education Media Project, www.eempc.org/lessons-of-the-loess-plateau.

MacGregor, Roy. "Heritage Lost." *Today Magazine*, Toronto Star.

Maclean, Dorothy. *Call of the Trees*. Lorian Press LLC, 2006.

Maclean, Dorothy. *To Hear the Angels Sing*. Lorian Press LLC, 2008.

Maclean, Dorothy. *Memoirs of an Ordinary Mystic*. Lorian Press LLC, 2010.

Reij, Chris. "Re-greening the Sahel: The Success of Natural Tree Regeneration." www.agriculturesnetwork.org. November 2012.

Simard, Suzanne. "Interspecies Cooperation" and "Mother Trees." Wikipedia, The Free Encyclopedia.

Spangler, David. *Partnering with Earth*. Lorian Press LLC, 2016.

Szekely, Edmond Bordeaux. *The Essene Teachings of Zarathustra*. International Biogenic Society, 1973.

Tompkins, Peter, and Christopher Bird. *The Secret Life of Plants*. Harper & Row, 1973.

Wohlleben, Peter. *The Hidden Life of Trees, What They Feel and How They Communicate*. Greystone Books, 2015.

About The Publisher

Lorian Press is a private, for profit business which publishes works approved by the Lorian Association. Current titles can be found on the Lorian website www.lorian.org. Our address is:

Lorian Press LLC
3935 Lakeridge Dr.
Holland, MI 49424

The Lorian Association is a not-for-profit educational organization. Its work is to help people bring the joy, healing, and blessing of their personal spirituality into their everyday lives. This spirituality unfolds out of their unique lives and relationships to Spirit, by whatever name or in whatever form that Spirit is recognized. The address is:

The Lorian Association
PO Box 1368
Issaquah, WA 98027

For more information, go to www.lorian.org
or www.lorianassociation.com

www.ingramcontent.com/pod-product-compliance
Lightning Source LLC
Chambersburg PA
CBHW072236270326
41930CB00010B/2149